Becoming a Scholarly Journal Editor

Becoming a Scholarly Journal Editor

Practical Advice for Editors and Tips for Authors

Wayne Journell

ROWMAN & LITTLEFIELD
Lanham • Boulder • New York • London

Published by Rowman & Littlefield
An imprint of The Rowman & Littlefield Publishing Group, Inc.
4501 Forbes Boulevard, Suite 200, Lanham, Maryland 20706
www.rowman.com
86-90 Paul Street, London EC2A 4NE, United Kingdom

British Library Cataloguing in Publication Information Available

Library of Congress Cataloging-in-Publication Data

Names: Journell, Wayne, author. Title: Becoming a scholarly journal editor : practical advice for editors and tips for authors / Wayne Journell.
Description: Lanham : Rowman & Littlefield, [2023] | Includes bibliographical references. | Summary: "This book serves as a guide for scholarly journal editors"— Provided by publisher.
Identifiers: LCCN 2022045490 (print) | LCCN 2022045491 (ebook) | ISBN 9781475867831 (cloth) | ISBN 9781475867848 (paperback) | ISBN 9781475867855 (epub)
Subjects: LCSH: Editing—Handbooks, manuals, etc. | Scholarly periodicals—Editing. | Scholarly periodicals—Authorship. | Scholarly publishing.
Classification: LCC PN162 .J68 2023 (print) | LCC PN162 (ebook) | DDC 808.02/7—dc23/eng/20220923
LC record available at https://lccn.loc.gov/2022045490
LC ebook record available at https://lccn.loc.gov/2022045491

Contents

Foreword

The editors of 12 scholarly journals interviewed by Jerry Wellington about their perception of the role of an editor led him to conclude that they saw themselves as "enhancers, improvers, disseminators, shapers of a field, mentors and mediators."[1] Wayne Journell personifies all these facets of the complex role of journal editor. Novice journal editors (and possibly the more experienced, too) as well as prospective authors will benefit enormously from the mentorship that this book offers.

I recall that my "training" as an editor for a well-regarded journal in my field over a decade ago consisted of a quick session on how to use the online system for managing reviews. All the "real stuff," I figured out "on the job." How I would have loved to have been taken on Journell's guided, "behind the scenes" tour of the everyday life of a journal editor. Editing an academic journal involves a set of occluded routines and practices that draw largely on implicit, procedural knowledge involving evaluation and appraisal, leading to, at times, fairly complex decision-making. Having reflected on his experience as long-term editor of *Theory & Research in Social Education*, Journell has managed to successfully distil the tacit knowledge gained into an eminently readable, wise, and judicious text in which he makes explicit what would otherwise remain hidden. The "implications for authors" sections that conclude chapters 2–5 should be mandatory reading for all early career scholars seeking to publish their work.

Although I would count myself as an experienced editor and have co-authored a book on writing for scholarly publication, I have found much to think about in terms of my own practice which I hope to apply to the *Journal of English for Research Publication Purposes* (published by John Benjamins), a new journal I have founded with a colleague. The section in chapter 2 weighing the pros and cons of special issues and the provision of clear guidelines will be extremely helpful. I particularly like the idea of appointing a doctoral student as a "fourth reviewer" as a way of introducing "the next generation of scholars to the world of academic publishing." While their feedback does not "count" in the review decision-making, the author is given the student's feedback and the student is given access to the other reviews once the final decision is made. There are many other novel ideas in this book that I believe would be of interest to more experienced editors as well.

Acknowledging that editors are often perceived as gatekeepers who seek to exclude rather than include, Journell sees the role of editor in a more custodial light; his mission is to "move the field forward in new or significant directions." Of course, taking on this task does mean at times closing the gates to work that in his estimation "would not fare well under external review" or may have a "fatal flaw." Chapter 3's nuanced yet frank discussion of some of the more challenging issues that Journell has faced in identifying potential reviewers, dealing with authors' response to reviewer feedback, and making editorial decisions is a trove of wisdom that invites multiple visits. In particular, I need to highlight the detailed consideration given to addressing potential reviewer bias in matters of race, gender, sexuality, or other aspects of identity.

I was heartened to discover that Journell and I share what some may see as an overly persnickety approach to editorial responsibility post acceptance of a manuscript. As the large publishing corporations that house most of our journals demonstrate a lack of interest in copy editing, he steps into the role, engaging in what are sometimes several rounds of back and forth with authors to ensure the final version submitted is as polished as possible. After all, as he says in chapter 4, the buck stops with the editor!

An editor's life doesn't end with clicking the "Accept" button, either. In the age of social media, yet another editor role has emerged: online promoter. Journell concludes chapter 5 with strategies for editors to harness Facebook, Twitter, and other digital resources to raise awareness of a journal's latest offering. This section is a must-read for us all.

For those readers wondering whether they have what it takes to become a journal editor, chapter 1 ends with a list of the most important qualities of successful editors: high level organizational skills, an open mind, a visionary perspective that looks to shape the field, an empathetic disposition that values mentoring, and, for good measure, a thick skin and strong writing skills. Do not, however, be deterred if you feel you are lacking in one or more of these domains; armed with Journell's delightfully helpful book, you too can take on the custodianship of your chosen journal.

—Sue Starfield, Emeritus Professor, University of New South Wales, and co-author (with Brian Paltridge) of *Getting Published in Academic Journals: Navigating the Publication Process* (2016)

NOTE

1. Jerry Wellington, *Getting Published: A Guide for Lecturers and Researchers* (New York: RoutledgeFalmer, 2003), 75.

Preface

My foray into journal editing started during my doctoral program at the University of Illinois at Urbana–Champaign. I served as the managing editor for *Research in the Teaching of English* (*RTE*), a top-tier journal in language arts education. My title was a fancy term for proctoring the flow of communication between authors, reviewers, and editors. Authors would send their manuscripts to an *RTE* email address, and then I would forward them to the editors, who would then give me names of potential reviewers to contact. When the reviews came in, I would collate them and send them to the editor in charge of that particular manuscript, who would then write a decision letter.

Although I was never part of the decision-making process for *RTE*—language arts is not even my area of expertise—serving as managing editor was an eye-opening experience. For example, it quickly became evident that critical reviews were more prevalent than reviews recommending acceptance. Also, I learned early on that, for many reviewers, due dates are merely suggestions—and the passive aggressive hounding of delinquent reviewers via email during my time at *RTE* would serve me well later on!

Perhaps the most educative aspect of that managing editor position came from attending the weekly editors' meetings. At that time, *RTE* used a co-editor model with three scholars serving as co-equal editors. At those weekly meetings, I would listen to the three editors discuss the merits of manuscripts and debate whether they were worthy of acceptance. It was there that I learned a valuable lesson about academic publishing: it is not enough for a manuscript to be "good"; rather, it needs to show significance in order to be published in a top-tier journal.

After graduating, I took a faculty position at the University of North Carolina at Greensboro, and I began interacting with journals as an author. Like most new faculty members, I had publishing successes and failures, but one individual was instrumental to my development as a scholar—Patricia Avery, who was editor of *Theory & Research in Social Education* (*TRSE*), which is the leading empirical journal in the field of social studies education.

I did not know Pat personally at the time; however, through my submissions to *TRSE* and her subsequent comprehensive decision letters, Pat unknowingly became an invaluable mentor.

I later found out through conversations with colleagues that Pat gave every author that same level of attention. At a public celebration honoring Pat when she stepped down as editor, Jennifer Hauver, a colleague who entered the field at roughly the same time as I did, noted that Pat had "helped shape the next generation of social studies scholars." Given the prominence of *TRSE* in the field of social studies education, such a proclamation was not an exaggeration. It was that level of impact, both on my own career and the field of social studies education more broadly, that made me realize the positive effect an editor can have.

Rarely do nontenured faculty get the opportunity to serve in an editorial capacity, but two years into my time as an assistant professor, I came across a call for a feature editor position in a midrange journal, *Social Studies Research and Practice* (*SSRP*). I threw caution to the wind and applied; looking back, I probably was the only applicant they had. I met with the executive editor at a conference, and she offered me the position soon thereafter.

The section that I edited for *SSRP* was their "interdisciplinary feature." Each issue of the journal contained one interdisciplinary article that highlighted how social studies could be integrated with language arts, science, or mathematics. Given that *SSRP* only published three issues per year, the position was hardly demanding. However, I had free rein over assigning reviewers and making decisions when it came to the manuscripts under my purview.

Perhaps the best lesson from my time working for *SSRP* was the realization that I liked editing. I enjoyed providing feedback to authors, and I found the process of synthesizing reviewers' comments and constructing a narrative about a manuscript to be intellectually stimulating work that improved my own scholarship. Of course, I modeled my decision letters after those I had received from Pat, a practice that I maintain today.

Four years later, I was offered another editing opportunity. Still an assistant professor, I was asked to serve as an associate editor for *TRSE*. Naturally, I jumped at the chance to join the editorial team of the top journal in the field—even for no compensation! *SSRP* had been a great stepping stone, but *TRSE* was the "big leagues," so to speak. Although the fundamentals of the position were the same—selecting reviewers, synthesizing reviews, and writing decision letters—both the workload and notoriety increased substantially.

The position made me considerably more visible in the field—although not immediately; at my first *TRSE* editorial board meeting, a senior scholar thought I was a representative from the publishing company! I was now interacting with "big names" as authors and reviewers on a regular basis, which was initially nerve-wracking, especially for someone who was about to apply for tenure. Yet, the time spent as associate editor of *TRSE* was invaluable; not only did I gain more experience editing, but I also was privy to the inside information that came from serving on the *TRSE* editorial team. Being able to access publisher's reports and work with the editorial team on efforts to increase the visibility of the journal was eye-opening.

I remained an associate editor for two years, and then in 2016, the editor's position opened. I applied, but I did not realistically think I had much of a shot. While I had been tenured by this point, *TRSE* editors in the past had typically been full professors. To this day, I have no idea if I was the first choice or the only person who ended up agreeing to do the work, but I ultimately landed the job (and, for the first time, received payment for my editorial work!). I have remained *TRSE* editor since then, recently becoming the first person to serve more than two terms.[1]

THEORY & RESEARCH IN SOCIAL EDUCATION

Given that the recommendations in this book come primarily from my time as *TRSE* editor, some context about the journal is needed. *TRSE* is the official journal of the College and University Faculty Assembly (CUFA) of the National Council for the Social Studies (NCSS). The CUFA Executive Board chooses the *TRSE* editor and oversees the journal; however, all decisions about journal content rest with the editor.

The journal was founded in 1973 and had humble beginnings. It took five years for the journal to become a quarterly publication, and even then, it was read almost exclusively by CUFA members.[2] *TRSE* remained an "in-house" publication that was published and distributed by NCSS until 2012. At that point, NCSS signed a contract with Taylor & Francis, an international publishing company, although CUFA retained editorial control and copyright over published articles.[3]

The move to Taylor & Francis vastly increased the visibility of the journal. *TRSE* is now an international publication that is widely recognized as the premier empirical journal in the field of social studies education. The journal publishes 20 articles and 12 book/media reviews per year. As of this writing, *TRSE* receives approximately 200+ submissions per year, around 40% of which are submitted by authors living outside of the United States. The current acceptance rate is around 10%.

The journal achieved a significant milestone in 2019 when it was selected for inclusion in Clarivate's Social Science Citation Index, becoming the first journal in the field of social studies education to receive that distinction. As a result, *TRSE* received an official impact factor and an increase in submissions. The journal's most recent (2021) impact factor was 3.256, and its 2021 CiteScore was 5.7, both of which place it as top journal in the field of educational research (more details about impact factors and CiteScores can be found in chapter 5). In 2021, *TRSE* articles were downloaded over 102,000 times by scholars located all around the world.

Not all journals, of course, are comparable to *TRSE*. As a disciplinary-specific journal, *TRSE* does not receive as many submissions as more generalist research journals, which may receive 800+ submissions per year. At the same time, as a top-tier research journal, *TRSE* likely attracts more attention than most midrange journals, practitioner journals, or regional journals. While different categories of journals have their respective challenges, the recommendations made in this book are going to be largely applicable to all types of scholarly journals.[4]

PURPOSE OF THE BOOK

Along with the infamous "Reviewer 2," journal editors are a leading cause of angst among scholars. Just mention the word "editor" to a group of scholars, and one is guaranteed to hear more horror stories than words of admiration. Whether it is due to excessively long review times or poor/minimal feedback to authors, editors often become the targets of authors' ire, and for good reason. Editors, unlike reviewers, are the visible faces of a journal, and more importantly, they are gatekeepers whose actions have real-life consequences for authors. When editors are bad at their jobs, careers are damaged, reputations of journals suffer, and the overall scholarship within a field is weakened.

The question driving this book is "why are there so few good journal editors out there?" There are a number of possible answers to that question, starting with the fact that journal editing is often a low-pay, largely thankless responsibility. This book, however, is focused on a less-acknowledged fact about the journal editing process—that there is rarely any official training for how to be a journal editor. Editors are typically leading scholars in their respective fields, but that alone does not guarantee that they will be effective managers of a journal. Even well-published scholars may face a steep learning curve when it comes to providing quality feedback to authors and navigating all of the intricacies of journal editing.

This book, then, is intended primarily to be a guide for scholarly journal editors. Irrespective of one's academic discipline or the size of one's journal, all editors have comparable responsibilities and deal with similar issues. Chapter 1 poses the question of why anyone would want to become a journal editor, discusses the discuss pros and cons of editing, and outlines the qualities that make an effective editor. Chapter 2 covers the decisions that editors must make even before the first manuscript is submitted—developing an editorial vision, choosing an editorial board, establishing reviewer timelines and procedures, and defining the types of decisions that will be rendered.

Chapters 3 and 4 cover processing submitted manuscripts. The former focuses on desk rejects and assigning reviewers; the latter covers making editorial decisions following peer review and writing decision letters. Chapter 5 discusses copyediting, the promotion of accepted articles, and ways to increase a journal's visibility. This chapter also explains various metrics designed to measure the health of a journal, such as its impact factor.

A secondary purpose of this book is to provide authors with a peek inside the process of journal editing. Most scholars are familiar with the nuts and bolts of the publishing process—manuscripts get sent out for external review and editors make decisions—but many lack a nuanced understanding of what goes on behind the scenes that may influence how an editor ultimately makes a publication decision.

By better understanding the types of decisions that editors make in terms of structuring and managing a journal, authors can make more informed decisions about which journals to target and how to respond to editorial feedback. Therefore, starting with chapter 2, each chapter ends with an "Implications for Authors" section that provides publication tips based on the content from that chapter.

NOTES

1. *TRSE* editors serve three-year terms with an option for subsequent three-year terms if reappointed by the CUFA Executive Board. From 1973–1995, no editor served more than one three-year term. However, the three editors who served from 1996–2013, Wayne Ross, Elizabeth Washington, and Patricia Avery, served two terms each. I had no idea that editors could serve more than two terms, but the CUFA bylaws do not specifically prohibit it. As such, the CUFA Executive Board reappointed me for a third term in 2021, which barring unforeseen circumstances, will be my last.

2. Paul E. Binford and Seth Eisworth, "The Growing Gap: The Origin of *Theory & Research in Social Education*," *Theory & Research in Social Education* 41, no. 4 (2013): 457–75, https://doi.org/10.1080/00933104.2013.840755; Jack L. Nelson and William B. Stanley, "Critical Studies and Social Education: 40 Years of *TRSE*," *Theory & Research in Social Education* 41, no. 4 (2013): 438–56, https://doi.org/10.1080/00933104.2013.842598.

3. Patricia G. Avery, "From the Editor," *Theory & Research in Social Education* 41, no. 4 (2013): 581–82, https://doi.org/10.1080/00933104.2013.858579.

4. The challenges specific to editing top academic journals, midrange journals, and global journals are unpacked in greater detail elsewhere. See, for example, Haridimos

Tsoukas, "Developing a Global Journal: Embracing Otherness," in *Opening the Black Box of Editorship,* ed. Yehuda Baruch, Alison M. Konrad, Herman Aguinis, and William H. Starbuck (New York: Palgrave MacMillan, 2008), 167–75; Theresa M. Welbourne, "Editing a Bridge Journal," in *Opening the Black Box of Editorship,* ed. Yehuda Baruch, Alison M. Konrad, Herman Aguinis, and William H. Starbuck (New York: Palgrave MacMillan, 2008), 157–66; and Sheldon Zedeck, "Editing a Top Academic Journal," in *Opening the Black Box of Editorship,* ed. Yehuda Baruch, Alison M. Konrad, Herman Aguinis and William H. Starbuck (New York: Palgrave MacMillan, 2008), 145–56. Also, if one is interested in creating a new scholarly journal from scratch, please see Larry J. Williams, "Reflections on Creating a New Scholarly Journal: Perspectives from a Founding Editor," in *Opening the Black Box of Editorship,* ed. Yehuda Baruch, Alison M. Konrad, Herman Aguinis, and William H. Starbuck (New York: Palgrave MacMillan, 2008), 188–96.

Acknowledgments

Writing a book is often viewed as a solitary endeavor, but in actuality, there are always many people who play important roles in either getting the project off the ground or making the final product stronger. I would like to thank the crew at Rowman & Littlefield, particularly Carlie Wall, for agreeing to publish a book that was out of my normal comfort zone of writing about social studies research. This book marks my fourth collaboration with Rowman & Littlefield, and I am profoundly grateful for how they have positively impacted my career.

I am indebted to Sue Starfield for lending her voice for the foreword, as well as Chezare Warren for allowing me to use the letter he shared on Twitter. I am also thankful to Aaron Bodle, Emma Thacker, and Jon Wargo for allowing me to publish the decision letters they received from me as editor of *Theory & Research in Social Education* (*TRSE*). As always, my wife, Kitrina, and my daughter, Hadleigh, deserve a great deal of thanks for their support at home and constant encouragement.

I would not have been able to write this book without the members of the executive board of the College and University Faculty Assembly (CUFA) of the National Council for the Social Studies over the years who have allowed me to serve as editor of *TRSE*. I am particularly beholden to the 2015–2016 CUFA executive board that initially entrusted me with the editorship. I doubt I was their first choice, but I have greatly appreciated being their final one. The subsequent executive boards have all been extremely supportive as well, which certainly makes my job easier.

Finally, although there are too many to individually name, I would like to formally thank the members of my *TRSE* editorial team and editorial board, as well as all of the authors and reviewers with whom I have interacted in an editorial capacity over the years. This book would not exist without them. I am grateful for the collegiality that you have shown me, even when we have disagreed. It is my hope that those who read this book might enjoy the same editorial experience that I have been fortunate to have while editing *TRSE*.

Chapter 1

Why Would Anyone Want to Be a Journal Editor?

I've spent a considerable amount of time as an editor. I've rejected about 2,500 papers, and accepted 200. No one likes a rejection and less than 1% consider it justified. Fortunately, there is some duplication across authors, so I have only made around 1,800 enemies.[1]

The above quotation from R. Preston McAfee, former editor of *The American Economist*, was made in jest, but there is some truth behind it. Similar to when faculty members transition into administrative roles, after becoming a journal editor, one often notices a change in the way their colleagues interact with them. While "enemies" might be an exaggeration, editors definitely become one of "them" once they start making publication decisions. Given that most top-tier journals have acceptance rates of less than 20%, editors wind up delivering more bad news than good, which can certainly strain relationships and create awkward moments at conferences.

Then there is also the increased workload to consider. Even when done poorly, editing a journal is time consuming. When done right, it can take up a considerable amount of time that could otherwise be spent on one's other professional responsibilities or trying to achieve that "work/life balance" that everyone dreams about. When people seek positions that require greater scorn and more work, they usually do it for the money, but that typically is not the case with journal editing. While some editors may receive a stipend for their work, it usually is not much, and there are certainly easier ways to earn extra spending money.[2]

At the end of the day, though, *someone* has to edit journals in order for academic publishing to continue. Yet, it is often not immediately clear why anyone would voluntarily agree to take on this type of work. Certainly, editing a journal can look impressive on one's curriculum vita, but most journal editors have already cleared the hurdles of promotion and tenure, so padding one's vita likely is not going to be an effective selling point. This chapter, then, offers other reasons to take on the responsibilities of journal editing while also acknowledging the opportunity costs of doing so.

THE BENEFITS OF JOURNAL EDITING

A social studies education colleague, Joel Westheimer, often tells the story of a preservice teacher who, when asked on an interview why he wants to be a K–12 teacher, responds by saying "power, prestige, and money." The answer is obviously a joke, but it serves as a creative conversation starter that ultimately leads to the preservice teacher landing the job. Westheimer, though, uses the story to make a broader point about teaching—that although the prestige and money are obviously farcical reasons why one would want to become a teacher, the ability of teachers to change lives suggests that there is some truth behind the power of teaching.[3]

A similar analogy can be made about journal editing. If one goes into editing expecting money and prestige, they are likely going to be disappointed. Editing, however, is powerful. It is this power that can provide the intrinsic motivation needed to engage in this type of work that is too often devoid of extrinsic rewards.

Before continuing, it is important to define the use of "power" in this context. By accepting and rejecting manuscripts, editors wield a certain amount of power over authors' careers and, by extension, their personal lives. That type of power, however, should not be a motivating factor in one's decision to become an editor. If one chooses to become an editor because making or destroying someone's livelihood excites them, then they have definitely entered editing for the wrong reasons (and they probably should take a critical look in the mirror).

The true power in editing comes in the ability to shape the scholarly direction of one's field. Editors are gatekeepers. For the individual scholar, that gate-keeping role is inherently personal, which is why editors often get characterized in a negative light. As Beth Luey, former editor of *Publishing Research Quarterly* noted, "When one's article is accepted, the image [of an editor] is of the kindly doorkeeper, opening the way to publication. When an article is rejected, the editor is the evil troll lurking under the bridge, barring the way."[4]

Authors, however, often fail to see the forest for the trees. The true responsibility of an editor lies in how the scholarship published in a journal moves a field forward in new or significant directions. When research of poor quality or middling interest to the field makes it into the pages of a journal, it is, at best, a waste of precious page space that could be given to stronger, more dynamic research and, at worst, damaging to a field of study.[5] This gate-keeping function of editing is of particular importance for the top journals in any given field.[6] The research published in those journals has the potential to influence policy and dramatically shift the direction of scholarship within their respective fields.

When thought about in this way, journal editing is a form of professional citizenship, and in most cases, an editor's influence on the field via editing will exceed that of their personal scholarship.[7] As of this writing, there have been over 120 articles published in *TRSE* during my editorship, many of which have become foundational, highly cited pieces for the field of social studies education. More importantly, all of them look substantially different from when they were initially submitted. The editing process is what leads to the final, published articles that influence policymakers and get cited by other scholars. The quality of research in any given field is beholden to this behind-the-scenes work of editors.

Even moving beyond the service to the field aspect of editing, there are other intrinsic motivations for becoming an editor. Editing provides an opportunity to work with authors and engage in scholarly mentoring. Although negative interactions with authors do happen, they are rare; most of the time, authors are grateful for feedback on their work, even if their manuscript is rejected.

This mentorship aspect of editing is especially important when dealing with novice scholars. It does not take much time editing a journal to realize that many doctoral students are not being adequately mentored on how to write scholarly research articles. In those cases, editors can be pivotal to a scholar's professional development. There are few aspects of editing more rewarding than taking a chance on a rough initial submission from a junior scholar and helping them mold it into a solid manuscript that is ultimately accepted for publication.

Of course, it would be disingenuous to pretend that all motivating factors to become an editor are intrinsic. Being a journal editor, particularly of a top-tier research journal, is prestigious, and for those still navigating the tenure track, it often is a compelling argument for promotion. After taking an editorial position, one's professional profile increases. Editing likely leads to more publication opportunities, as well as invited talks and panel sessions at conferences. For good or bad, editors are noticed, and there is inherent professional value in being a recognizable figure within one's field.

Journal editing is also arguably the best scholarly professional development one can receive. Helping others remedy deficiencies in their manuscripts inevitably makes editors more aware of weaknesses in their own work. In a survey of journal editors, Yehuda Baruch noted that one participant reported that they "published much more [of their own work]" after having the experience of serving as a journal editor and that it took "less time (less revisions) to get them [published]," which suggests that "editorship experience bears fruits, which may ripen at a later stage."[8] Also, few people are going to be as knowledgeable of their field as the editors of a top-tier journal. They will be privy to new trends in the field before anyone else, which can also stimulate ideas for one's own research.

In short, a case can be made for taking on the responsibility of journal editing. However, there are opportunity costs of doing so, and editing may not be suitable for all types of scholars. The rest of this chapter discusses those opportunity costs and describes the types of professional dispositions one needs to be successful as a journal editor.

OPPORTUNITY COSTS OF JOURNAL EDITING

Outside of the potential for strained relationships with colleagues mentioned earlier, there are other professional opportunity costs of journal editing that must be considered. The time that editing takes, especially if done correctly, will likely hurt one's own research productivity. With all of the demands placed on faculty, particularly tenured faculty with multiple service obligations, finding time to collect data and write is already difficult. The constant work of journal editing—selecting reviewers, sending out reviewer reminders, writing decision letters—encroaches on that already scarce time.

Not surprisingly, then, in that aforementioned survey of journal editors, Baruch found that nearly half (43%) felt that they published less than they did prior to becoming an editor.[9] As one might expect, the most cited reason for the decline in research productivity was a lack of time. As one editor commented, "I had so much to read as an editor that was unrelated to my own work that I had no time left for my own research."[10]

Becoming a journal editor also narrows one's options in terms of publication outlets. Since publishing in the journal that one edits is a morally questionable practice (see next chapter), it means that journal editors have fewer outlets at their disposal for their own work. In larger fields with multiple top-tier journals, the loss of one journal as a potential publication outlet may not be a concern. However, in smaller, more specialized fields, removing a prominent journal from consideration for one's own work may be problematic, as it could force editors to attempt to publish their own work in more generalist outlets or in other venues (e.g., book chapters) that may not hold as much prestige.

The inability to publish in one's journal may also limit opportunities to collaborate with others. It is important for editors to be up front about their publishing limitations prior to engaging in collaborative projects. One would not want to prevent junior faculty or graduate students from publishing their work in a top-tier journal because the editor of the journal is a co-author on a manuscript. Of course, editors could always remove their names from a piece in order to allow others to publish in their journal, but doing so would mean that the editor would receive no recognition for their work if the manuscript eventually was published.

Finally, committing to serve a term as a journal editor may preclude one from being able to take advantage of other professional opportunities. While it is theoretically possible to hold an administrative position (e.g., department chair, dean) while editing a journal, it is not advisable. Although journal editing requires many of the same skills as university administrative work, and thus could be considered good preparation, oftentimes editors will have to choose one or the other.

QUALITIES OF SUCCESSFUL JOURNAL EDITORS

After weighing the pros and cons of being an editor, there is another element to consider before accepting a position as a journal editor. In addition to scholarly expertise, editing also requires certain dispositions. Here is a list of the most important qualities of successful journal editors:

Organized

Perhaps the most important personal quality an editor can have is being organized. Journal editing is ideal for type A personalities who adhere to deadlines, are responsive to emails, and can manage time effectively. As long as one stays on top of the workload, the work of journal editing is manageable. Once one falls behind, however, it can become almost impossible to dig out of that hole because the submissions never stop.

Staying on top of the workload requires understanding that journal editing is not something that can be regulated to once or twice a week. Editors do not necessarily write decision letters on a daily basis, but for most journals, chances are that editors will need to spend at least some part of each working day doing editorial work. On some days, that work may only take 20–30 minutes (e.g., checking for tardy reviewers and sending reminders); other days, it may take an hour or two (e.g., reading submissions, assigning reviewers, writing desk rejects, promoting articles on social media); and occasionally, it may take an entire morning/afternoon (e.g., writing extensive decision letters).

Being able to plan ahead is essential to being a successful editor. Submissions tend to come in waves—the end of summer and winter breaks, the end of semesters, and immediately following conferences—which means that editorial work also comes in waves. When a manuscript is initially submitted, there is not that much work involved; doing an initial read and selecting reviewers does not take that much time. The time-consuming work begins weeks later when all of the reviews come in. Therefore, planning ahead—both with the work of the journal and one's own teaching, research, service, and personal obligations—is necessary.

Ideologically Open

Editors are scholars who come to the position with a well-established research profile and certain expectations for what constitutes quality scholarship. It is impossible to completely divorce oneself from those beliefs, but at the same time, editors must understand that the journal is not theirs. For the health of the field, it is important that editors are ideologically open to frameworks, methodologies, and concepts that deviate from those with which they are comfortable or believe to be "correct."

Visionary

Editors also need to approach the position with a vision of what the journal could become. That vision could pertain to the types of manuscripts that the journal publishes or ways in which the journal could make a greater impact on policy. Editorial visions are discussed in greater depth in the next chapter, but it is important that prospective editors have a disposition that is accepting of change. Taking an editorial position to maintain the status quo does little to push a field in new or significant directions.

Empathetic

As an editor, it is important to never forget the feeling of having one's manuscript rejected. Given that editors dispense more bad news than good, maintaining an empathetic tone with authors is necessary. Getting rejected is a reality of academia, but a rejection should not leave authors feeling demoralized. Especially for doctoral students and tenure-earning faculty members, a rejection letter that also highlights the strengths of the manuscript can go a long way toward maintaining their confidence as a scholar.

Editors have the luxury of looking at manuscripts from a dispassionate lens. They are concerned about the corpus of manuscripts that are submitted to a journal, not any specific individual submission. Authors, however, are heavily invested in each individual submission; in the "publish or perish" atmosphere of academia, one publication may make the difference when it comes to promotion and tenure.

As such, emails asking "can you give me a status update on my manuscript?" or "how long is the typical review time for this journal?" can get annoying, but they are understandable. While it may be tempting to respond with a snarky comment like "you will get a decision once the reviewers actually submit their responses," a more empathetic response will help assuage authors' fears and increase the likelihood that they submit future manuscripts to the journal.

That empathetic tone should also transfer to interactions with potential authors. Some potential authors will ask editors to look over abstracts, or even full papers, to see if their work might be a good fit for the journal. While no editor has time to give all potential manuscripts an initial read, if an author emails politely/sincerely, it is usually worth giving the abstract/manuscript a cursory read to at least see if it is within the scope of the journal, albeit with the caveat that an editor cannot guarantee acceptance without the manuscript undergoing peer review.

Disposition for Mentoring

Along with empathy, editors should have a disposition for mentoring. As noted earlier, editing has the potential to improve the scholarship within a field, but only if an editor *wants* to engage in that type of mentoring model. Writing decision letters that not only evaluate the merits and limitations of a manuscript, but also offer suggestions for how authors can improve their craft takes considerable time and energy. Editors should want to embrace the educative potential of their positions and, in many cases, serve as the scholarly mentors that many faculty members did not have in their doctoral programs.

Strong Writers

It is a popular misconception that people who write for a living must be exceptional writers. One lesson that editors quickly learn is that just because someone has received a doctorate and written a dissertation does not mean that they use proper grammar or sentence structure. Moreover, if one is editing an international journal that receives submissions from authors whose mother tongue is different than the language used by the journal, many of those international submissions need quite a bit of work in terms of language conventions.

As will be discussed in chapter 5, editors are the first copyeditors of accepted manuscripts, and oftentimes that responsibility requires rewriting portions of a manuscript in order to make it grammatically correct. As such, it is imperative that editors are strong technical writers. The process of editing will make all editors better writers than they were before taking the position, but strong copyediting skills are necessary at the outset.

Thick Skin

Most of the talk around developing thick skin in academia is targeted at authors. Editors, however, also need to learn not to take criticism personally. It is a popular practice for scholars to complain about their publishing experiences on social media, and oftentimes those experiences are exaggerated or misinformed. Authors may, for example, complain publicly that their manuscript was rejected by an editor because the journal is not accepting of a particular methodology, framework, or ontological perspective when, in reality, the reviewers told the editor privately that the manuscript was simply not very good.

Similarly, it can be frustrating when editors hear that a journal or field refuses to publish certain topics or that a journal is not welcoming of diverse perspectives when the editor knows that the journal has not received many submissions in those areas. In such cases, editors have to stay silent and just absorb the criticism. Unfortunately, that type of restraint comes with the job. Trying to contradict such criticism is often a pointless endeavor since much of the evidence that editors have at their disposal is confidential.

In short, editing a journal is not for everyone, but for those who have the right dispositions, it can be a rewarding experience. The rest of this book offers advice on the practical aspects of editing. The less that editors must learn through trial and error, the more rewarding the experience will likely be.

NOTES

1. R. Preston McAfee, "Edifying Editing," *The American Economist* 55, no. 1 (2010): 1. https://doi.org/10.1177%2F056943451005500101.

2. For reference, I could teach two summer courses at my university and make approximately the same amount of money as I do editing *TRSE*, and the summer courses would require considerably less time!

3. Joel Westheimer, "The Power of Education," last modified February 9, 2009, https://www.youtube.com/watch?v=DX1YC5BwGSI.

4. Beth Luey, "The Profession of Journal Editing," *Profession* 2009, no. 1 (2009): 112.

5. James Galipeau et al., "Systematic Review of the Effectiveness of Training Programs in Writing for Scholarly Publication, Journal Editing, and Manuscript Peer Review," *Systematic Reviews* 2, no. 1 (2013): 1–7.

6. Luey, "The Profession," 115.

7. Ann Marie Ryan, "How May I Help You? Editing as Service," in *Opening the Black Box of Editorship,* ed. Yehuda Baruch, Alison M. Konrad, Herman Aguinis, and William H. Starbuck (New York: Palgrave MacMillian, 2008), 30–31.

8. Yehuda Baruch, "Opening the Black Box of Editorship: Editors' Voice," in *Opening the Black Box of Editorship,* ed. Yehuda Baruch, Alison M. Konrad, Herman Aguinis, and William H. Starbuck (New York: Palgrave MacMillian), 217–218.

9. Baruch, "Opening the Black Box," 217. It is worth noting, however, that 17% of editors in Baruch's study actually said that they published more during their editorships than before.

10. Baruch, "Opening the Black Box," 217.

Chapter 2

Getting Started

Developing the Structure of the Journal

Many of the decisions that directly relate to the success of a journal are made before the first manuscript is submitted. If editors can develop solid structures and policies at the outset of their editorship, then fewer problems will arise in the years that follow. This chapter covers many of the initial decisions that editors must make, starting with their editorial vision.

DEVELOPING AN EDITORIAL VISION

As discussed in the previous chapter, one should not apply for an editorial position without a vision for what the journal should become. An editorial vision is obviously going to be journal-specific and respond to the needs of a particular field. A new editor offers the chance for a reset; thus, an editorial vision should explain how the editorship will seek to move the field's scholarship in a new direction.

In many ways, editorial visions are similar to promises that politicians make on the campaign trail in that they are aspirational but largely out of the politicians' control should they be elected. Just because an editor wants more manuscripts on certain topics, there is no guarantee it will happen. However, just like in politics, if there is no attempt to make a change, it is almost guaranteed that the status quo will remain in place. It also stands to reason that if readers of the journal are not aware of the editorial vision, then it likely will be ineffective. Therefore, it is a good practice to include a "from the editor" piece in the first issue under one's editorship that outlines one's vision.

What, then, should an editorial vision cover? The first aspect of an editorial vision is ideological. What topics and methodologies will the journal entertain? Are there certain topics or methodologies that have historically been marginalized within a field and should be brought to the forefront? In most fields, there is no shortage of possible topics of importance; therefore, it is essential that editors prioritize. Providing a laundry list of marginalized topics is less effective than clearly identifying a handful of the most pressing issues in a field and encouraging submissions in those areas.

Editorial visions are similar to the "elevator description" of one's dissertation that they must have prepared before going to campus interviews. If one cannot articulate their ideological vision in a handful of paragraphs, then it likely means that the vision is not specific enough. Moreover, most authors are not likely going to read a lengthy thesis on the state of the field; they simply want to know if their work is of interest to the journal.

To give an idea of what an editorial vision might look like, here is the section from my initial "from the editor" piece that outlined the ideological vision that my editorial team sought for *TRSE*:

One aspect of our editorial vision is to increase the ideological and methodological diversity of the scholarship published in *TRSE*. There will always be a place for case studies of classroom practices and discussions of civic education and historical thinking in the journal, but we would like to see those topics regularly accompanied by articles pertaining to other relevant but underresearched aspects of our field. At a minimum, we would love to see more scholarship pertaining to topics and issues that practitioners regularly encounter but have traditionally not been featured in the pages of *TRSE*, such as the teaching of economics, geography, psychology, and sociology in K–12 schooling, or the teaching of social studies in particular contexts, such as early childhood education, elementary education, or inclusive and bilingual classrooms. We also believe that there is inherent value in research conducted by scholars who may lie on the periphery of social studies education (e.g., historians, political scientists, economists, geographers) and scholars who may not identify as social studies educators but whose work impacts our field (e.g., scholars focusing on diversity in K–12 education, teacher educators). There are natural connections to be made between those disciplines and the work of social studies educators, and we would welcome submissions that bridge these traditional divides.

Methodologically, scholarship published in *TRSE* tends to be predominantly qualitative in nature. On one hand, the preponderance of qualitative research in *TRSE* is not problematic . . . On the other hand, we believe that *TRSE* should be at the forefront of policy decisions related to social studies education, and the inclusion of more quantitative and mixed-method scholarship would help ensure that the work published in the journal influences those decisions.

Another goal that we have is to continue the increased attention to diversity that has been present in *TRSE* over the past decade . . . Yet we can always do more. Even within this aspect of the literature, some topics are even more underrepresented than others. Over the past decade, for example, *TRSE* articles centered on race/ethnicity have tended to focus on the experience of African American students and teachers or the representation of African Americans within the social studies curriculum. While we certainly have more to learn about the experiences of African American students and teachers, particularly in light of movements, such as Black Lives Matter, that have increased awareness to racial injustice in the United States, our field is also in need of more research on the experiences of other people of color in social studies classrooms. Similarly, the increased amount of research on the experiences of lesbian, gay, bisexual, and transgender (LGBT) students in social studies classrooms has tended to focus primarily on the LGB portion of the acronym. Issues related to the experiences of transgender students and teachers in social studies classrooms remain vastly underresearched, particularly within the pages of *TRSE*. We urge the field to continue exploring the ways *all* students and educators interact with the social studies curriculum, and *TRSE* will remain a venue for that scholarship.

Finally, we seek to continue the efforts of previous editorial teams in terms of marketing *TRSE* as an international publication . . . In 2016, approximately 30% of submissions came from authors residing outside of the United States . . . We believe that international perspectives on social education contribute to a more robust understanding of pertinent issues in our field, and we look forward to increased international submissions in the future.[1]

Have all of those goals come to fruition? No. Some have; *TRSE* has become even more international in scope, and the journal has received a greater number of articles on race in recent years. Yet, there remains a dearth in submissions on economics, geography, and psychology education, and the journal has yet to receive a submission related specifically to transgender issues in social studies education.

Politicians are often judged on whether they fulfill their campaign promises; should editors be assessed on how well their editorial visions become reality? Editors can take some steps to encourage manuscripts on specific topics (e.g., making explicit calls for manuscripts, publishing special issues, encouraging authors at conferences to submit to the journal), and they can also give deference in the decision-making process to manuscripts that focus on marginalized topics (e.g., giving an author a chance to revise and resubmit instead of issuing a reject decision). Yet, all editors can really do is offer encouragement, and ultimately their editorial vision is reliant on the field to respond through its scholarship. Editors should not feel like failures if all aspects of their vision do not materialize; even marginal changes can have long-lasting impacts on a field.

Where editors have more control is in the enactment of the practical side of their editorial vision. Ideological goals are important, but so are goals related to the functioning and visibility of the journal. When submitting manuscripts to a journal, authors expect a reasonable review time and constructive feedback. Then, if they are fortunate enough to have their manuscript published, authors hope that people read and cite their work.

By some estimates, a large percentage of academic articles are not read by more than a handful of people.[2] The digitalization of academic articles and the rise of online journals means that consumers of research have more options for scholarly information than ever before. Therefore, it is essential that journals find ways to stick out in the crowded academic publishing environment.

Chapter 5 will discuss specific ways to promote journals and highlight articles, but the point to be made here is that an editorial vision should also encompass ways to broaden the readership and influence of the journal. In many ways, the ideological and promotional aspects of one's editorial vision are connected; if authors—including the ones doing work on topics that mesh with an editor's ideological vision—believe that their work will reach a larger audience by publishing in a certain journal, then they are more likely to submit their work to that journal.

In short, an editorial vision is essential to the success of a journal. This vision should be established prior to any other major decisions because, as will be explained in the remainder of this chapter, a journal's staffing and editorial policies will be shaped by both the types of manuscripts a journal hopes to receive and the author experience it intends to promote.

DETERMINING THE STRUCTURE OF THE JOURNAL

There is no absolutely "correct" way to structure a journal, and if someone is becoming an editor of an established journal, a certain amount of structure may already be in place. However, structure can change! There will be feature/research articles in every journal, but beyond that, there are many different options in terms of the types of content published.

Some journals publish book reviews, and some have additional sections that allow for commentary about specific aspects of the field. The journal, *PS: Political Science & Politics*, for example, has standing sections on "The Profession" and "The Teacher" in each issue, in addition to main research articles. They also publish symposia on specific topics in most issues.

There are benefits to having different types of publications beyond just peer-reviewed research articles in a journal. Book reviews, for example, can offer graduate students and early-career scholars easier opportunities to publish in top-tier journals, and more informal types of sections within a journal can lead to more diverse voices within the pages of a journal, particularly if commentary is solicited. Ultimately, how a journal is structured should be determined by the editorial vision and what role the journal has within a field. Some journals are intended only to disseminate research findings; others are meant to also serve as a place for commentary on a field.

For print-based journals, the various sections within a journal must be balanced with the page limits requested by the publisher (online journals have more leeway here). If there are going to be standing sections in every issue, then that may mean fewer research articles get published in each issue or that word/page limits for articles need to be reduced. Word/page limits are always a point of contention for authors, but the determination of those limits should be aligned with the editorial vision for the journal. If a journal is intended to be a top-tier empirical journal, then editors need to give authors enough room to navigate detailed methods sections and lengthy literature reviews.

TRSE, for example, is currently allotted 660 pages per volume by the publisher, which equates to approximately 165 pages per issue. Given that *TRSE* is an empirical journal, we give authors up to 10,000 words, excluding abstract, tables/figures, endnotes, and references, which is one of the of the lengthier word limits of journals in the field of educational research. Practitioner journals, however, often have much more restrictive word limits—often around 2,500 words—because the readers of those journals are not typically as interested in methodological details and do not have time to wade through lengthy articles.

The old saying is that "rules are made to be broken," and word/page limits are no exception. It is not unusual for articles published in *TRSE* to end up closer to 15,000 words, excluding abstract, tables/figures, endnotes, and references, by the time it is published. Reviewers almost always request additions and not deletions; therefore, flexibility is often a necessity. Keeping a fairly strict word limit at the time of submission, however, can help ensure that accepted manuscripts do not become unmanageable by the time the review process ends. Another way that *TRSE* allows for such lengthy research manuscripts is by being strict on the length of the book/media reviews that the journal publishes—no more than 3,500 words.

CONSTRUCTING AN EDITORIAL TEAM AND EDITORIAL BOARD

Editorial Teams

An editorial team is the small group of scholars who make editorial decisions on manuscripts or oversee certain sections of a journal. For example, *TRSE*'s editorial team is comprised of the editor, two associate editors, and a book/media review editor. Some journals have a co-editor model, and others may have many associate editors. Regardless of the size of the editorial team, they all serve at the pleasure of the editor, and generally, the editor has final say over content published in the journal.

There is no formula for determining the size of an editorial team. At a minimum, there should always be at least one associate editor who can handle manuscripts from authors who pose a conflict of interest for the editor (e.g., colleagues at the editor's university, an editor's doctoral advisor or doctoral advisees). Beyond that consideration, the decision comes down to the editorial vision of a journal, the number of manuscripts a journal receives, workload, and editorial consistency.

No editor can be experts in all aspects of a field, and few are proficient in all types of methodologies. It is important that editors are aware of their own scholarly limitations. If an editor's vision is to broaden the scope of the journal and be accepting of diverse perspectives and methodologies, then the choice of associate editors can help make that vision a reality. Moreover, choosing individuals who are known experts in certain perspectives or methodologies indicates to authors what kind of scholarship the journal will entertain.[3]

Too many associate editors, however, can create issues related to workload and editorial consistency. Particularly if associate editors are receiving payment from a publisher or an organization, there needs to be enough manuscript submissions so that all members of the editorial team are earning their keep. That said, editors are the main face of the journal, and when payments are involved, they typically get paid the most; therefore, they should almost always take the lion's share of submissions.

The other consideration when determining the number of associate editors is ensuring that authors have a similar experience regardless of which editor oversees their manuscript. Fewer associate editors typically mean greater editorial consistency.[4] Even if editors outline expectations about selectivity with their associate editors, the more of them that there are, the greater the likelihood that the journal's standards fluctuate, and such deviations quickly become known within the field. Journals never want to get to the point where authors are specifically requesting certain editors because they feel as though their manuscript has a greater chance of acceptance with them overseeing the review process.

If the journal has sections beyond research articles (e.g., book/media reviews), then finding someone to serve as editors of those sections can help reduce the editor's workload. Given that these sections often do not require external reviews and editorial decisions, they are ideal positions for junior scholars or scholars without prior editorial experience. However, the workload in these positions can be intense, and oftentimes these sections attract submissions from graduate students and early-career faculty that require extensive copyediting. Therefore, these section editors need the same time management and writing skills as the rest of the editorial team.

Editorial Boards

Editorial boards are comprised of scholars who do not make editorial decisions, but rather, they review a significant portion of submissions, and they provide oversight and counsel to the editor. Being named to an editorial board of a journal, particularly a top-tier research journal, is typically considered a prestigious honor that looks good on one's vita. As a result, it is usually not too difficult to find people willing to serve in this capacity.

Just because someone is willing to be on a journal's editorial board does not guarantee that they will be a useful board member. The primary responsibility of editorial board members is to complete reviews; therefore, it is important that editors select individuals who they know will provide detailed, constructive feedback to both editors and authors and who will complete their reviews on time. As will be discussed in the next chapter, hounding reviewers to complete their reviews consumes a great deal of an editor's time, so ensuring that the culprits are not members of the editorial board is essential to maintaining an editor's sanity.

Editorial board members should complete a large percentage of the reviews for the journal, again to maintain editorial consistency. All journals use ad hoc reviewers, but they can be undependable, and their feedback on manuscripts can be poor. At least one *TRSE* editorial board member serves as a reviewer on approximately 95% of submissions that go out for external review (and often, there are multiple board members on a single manuscript). This consistency in reviewer feedback—especially as editors become accustomed to how their editorial board members evaluate manuscripts—is invaluable, a point that will be elaborated on in chapter 4.

Given the number of reviews that editorial board members do, it is important for editors to be up front with their workload expectations.[5] For example, *TRSE* editorial board members are told to expect approximately four manuscript reviews per year; however, the actual number varies depending on the topics the journal receives. The editorial board members who are experts in history or civic education end up reviewing more manuscripts than the board members who are experts in geography and economics education.

It is important for editorial board members to know that they are not board members for life. Making the editorial board term one or two years with an option for renewal is an easy way to remove editorial board members who may not be fulfilling their obligations to the journal. However, there will occasionally be editorial board members who are not the most active reviewers but who still serve a purpose being on the board. As will be discussed in chapter 5, if a journal wants to apply for an impact factor, one of the requirements is to have "Editor and Editorial Board Member affiliations, geographic diversity, and publication records [that are] consistent with the stated scope and published content of the journal."[6]

In other words, journals need "big names" on their editorial boards, and in the case of international journals, scholars from other countries. The bigger the name, the more invitations they receive and the less time they can commit to any one aspect of their service profile. So, it is certainly possible that the labor of editorial boards is not distributed equally, but unfortunately that is one of the realities of academic publishing.

The inclusion of prominent scholars on editorial boards highlights another one of their functions—editorial board members are visible faces of a journal. Similar to the way editorial teams can highlight the ideological and methodological diversity of an editorial vision, the composition of editorial boards also sends a message to authors about what types of scholarship are valued in a journal. Editorial boards are also not static; if editors notice a growing subfield that is not represented on the editorial board, adding a prominent member of that subfield would hopefully signal that submissions on that topic would be welcome.

Of course, just like with editorial teams, editorial boards need to be manageable and be commiserate with the number of submissions that the journal receives. There is no formula other than to make sure that the number of submissions does not require most board members to review more than the number of manuscripts they agreed to when they took the position. To give some context, *TRSE* receives approximately 200 submissions per year, and there are currently 33 editorial board members. With that number, few board members actually review their four manuscripts per year, and most review two or three.

DEVELOPING EDITORIAL POLICIES

To outside observers, editing a journal may seem relatively straightforward; manuscripts are submitted, and decisions of acceptance or rejection are rendered. However, there are a number of other decisions that editors make on a regular basis, many of which contain ethical components. By setting clear editorial policies at the outset of their editorship, editors can avoid being caught off guard by unexpected questions or requests.

Determining Who Can Publish

As noted in the previous chapter, editors publishing their own scholarly work in the journal that they edit is an ethically questionable practice. While some reputable journals allow it, presumably with associate editors overseeing the external review process, it is not a good look. If authors perceive a journal to not be above board in their publication process, then it decreases the likelihood that they will publish there.

The question then becomes how far this policy should extend. Editorial team? Editorial board? There is no "right" answer to this question, but a strong case can be made that editorial team members should not be able to publish in the journal during their terms. There are two main reasons to take this stance.

First, associate editors often have administrative privileges in the online management system used by the journal; therefore, they may be privy to confidential information (e.g., the identities of scholars who reviewed their manuscripts) that would violate anonymous review procedures. Second, editors likely work closely with their editorial teams, which creates a conflict of interest and the potential to harm the team's working relationship should an associate editor's manuscript be rejected.

It is important that editors are explicit on this requirement when assembling their editorial team. In smaller fields, the inability to publish in a top journal may prevent someone from agreeing to take a position on the editorial team. Associate editors are often tenured, so it may be less of a concern for them, but that may not be the case for section editors or book/media review editors who may still be on the tenure track. Editors may make the decision to allow those junior scholars to submit manuscripts to the journal since they do not have the same level of informational access as associate editors, but it still creates the possibility of discord within the editorial team.

Editorial board members are different. They do not have access to journal management systems, nor do they make acceptance decisions on manuscripts. They work with editors but not to the same extent as the editorial team. Also, if one does not allow editorial board members to submit, editors are disqualifying a large number of highly influential scholars from submitting to the journal, which could negatively affect the quality of the journal's published content.

Another issue that arises occasionally is when scholars submit multiple manuscripts to a journal at the same time. Should they all get accepted, having multiple first-author articles by the same author published at once can give the appearance of impropriety. Editors can alleviate this concern by mandating that authors cannot publish multiple articles from the same dataset or instituting a policy stating that an author can only have one first-authored manuscript under external review at a time.

Invited Submissions

Although most journals rely on anonymous peer review to determine published content, some editors may also invite scholars to publish op-eds or theoretical articles from time to time. Invited submissions provide editors with more control over what topics are represented in the journal, and if they are penned by influential authors, they can be highly cited articles. Yet anytime editors allow non–peer-reviewed work into the journal, it raises potential ethical issues.

Invited submissions raise questions such as who decides which scholars get to write invited articles and how is the journal ensuring that invited submissions are reflective of the diversity within the field? It is for those reasons that *TRSE*'s policy is that all content, with the exception of solicited book/media reviews, undergoes peer review. However, in the event that editors choose to publish invited material, it is best practice to seek advice from the editorial team and editorial board on who should be invited to submit.

Special Issues

A related conundrum can be found in the question of whether to devote special issues of the journal to a specific topic. After accepting an editorial position, editors can expect to have colleagues approach them at conferences or via email with a "great idea for a special issue." Almost always, those great ideas just happen to coincide with the suggester's personal scholarly interests.

Similar to invited submissions, special issues are generally thought to lead to greater numbers of citations than regular issues, which can improve a journal's impact metrics.[7] They also allow a journal to focus on a specific topic that may have been under researched within a field. Depending on the topic, special issues can increase the diversity of authors who publish in the journal as well. Finally, if a journal is receiving fewer submissions than normal, a special issue is a way to increase submissions and help ensure that there are enough accepted articles to fill the pages of the journal.

Special issues, however, are a logistical nightmare; if there are guest editors, they have to be placed in editorial roles within the journal management system, and the journal is then processing two streams of manuscripts—one for the special issue and one for the regular submissions. Also, there is a risk that the guest editors will not maintain the same standards as the regular editorial team in terms of their evaluation of manuscripts.

Special issues also delay the publication process, which means that "regular" accepted manuscripts in the publication queue are not published as quickly as normal. Special issues are also risky; there is no guarantee that the journal will receive an adequate number of acceptable manuscripts to fill the special issue, and if that happens, the journal is forced to scrap the issue or accept substandard manuscripts.

Perhaps the greatest concern about special issues is ethical in nature. Most special issue topics narrow the pool of potential authors, which can be construed as being exclusionary. In other words, if a journal has a special issue on a certain topic, readers would be able to guess which scholars will be represented in most cases. Such exclusivity goes against the general belief of most editors that all potential authors be given an equal opportunity to publish in a journal.

To date, there have not been any special issues of *TRSE* in my editorship for the reasons given above. However, along with the *TRSE* editorial board, I developed guidelines for the consideration of special issues. Here are the main tenets:

- The topic should be of interest/concern for the field.
- The topic should be an underrepresented aspect of social education that has not appeared exclusively in *TRSE* or other journals typically read by *TRSE* readers.
- The topic should be broad enough that a variety of perspectives and potential authors would be considered for inclusion in the issue.
- The issue would adhere to *TRSE* standards for publication (i.e., anonymous peer review by at least three external reviewers).

Of course, the first three of those guidelines are subjective. As a result, we developed a rigorous procedure for approving special issues:

- Special issues will only be considered if doing so will not prevent accepted manuscripts in the queue from being published within one calendar year of acceptance.
- Members of the editorial team or the editorial board can submit proposals for a special issue, and the proposal would be presented at the first available meeting of the editorial board. It takes a 2/3 combined vote of the editorial team and editorial board to approve a special issue.
- If someone outside of the editorial team or editorial board proposes a special issue, the editor will serve as an initial screener and will have the option to "desk reject" any proposals as they see fit. If the editor determines the proposal to have merit, and it is logistically possible for a special issue to occur, the proposal would be presented at the first available meeting of the editorial board, and it would require a 2/3 combined vote of the editorial team and editorial board to approve the special issue.

- If a proposal for a special issue is accepted, the editorial board will determine whether the editor should oversee the production of the special issue or whether a guest editor(s) should be approached.
- The call for the special issue would need to be made at least 12 months before the issue is scheduled to be published.

In short, special issues can be beneficial if they are conceived in a thoughtful manner that is consistent with the editorial vision guiding the journal. This model used for *TRSE* is not necessarily one that can be replicated for all journals, but the takeaway point is that there should be oversight beyond just the whim of an editor in determining the viability of a special issue.

Right to Respond

Many journals allow readers the ability to respond, in writing, to articles published in the journal, and some make commentary about published articles a regular feature of the journal. When journals publish commentaries about articles, they typically also invite the authors of the original article to respond to the commentary. If editors recognize that an article may be edgy or prompt strong reactions, they may choose to be proactive and invite a scholar to respond so that the article, commentary, and response to the commentary are all published in the same issue. Oftentimes, however, the commentary is unsolicited and is published in an issue of the journal subsequent to that of the original article.

As with special sections of a journal, the value of commentary must be weighed against the page space they consume. Although commentaries are typically short (under 3,000 words) and responses to commentary even shorter (around 500 to 1000 words), if they become a regular feature of a journal, it could ultimately mean fewer articles or book reviews are able to be published. On the other hand, commentaries can stimulate productive conversations for the field, particularly on burgeoning or controversial topics, stances, or methods.

Unsolicited commentaries should undergo some form of editorial oversight, and it should be clear that not all commentaries will be published. However, anonymous peer review may not always be appropriate for this type of submission given that commentaries in response to published manuscripts often involve a public disagreement over a particular finding or stance taken in the original article (e.g., Scholar X publishes an article invalidating the findings of an earlier study by Scholar Y, prompting Scholar Y to submit a commentary suggesting that Scholar X is mistaken). Also, given the potential combative nature of commentaries, it is important that they are properly vetted to ensure that the argument is based on philosophical disagreements and not personal animosity.[8]

At *TRSE*, we developed two criteria for the consideration of commentaries. First, the commentary must respond to an article published within the previous calendar year. Second, all commentaries would be sent to a member of the editorial board who is an expert in that area of scholarship. The editorial board member would provide a deanonymized (i.e., they would know the identity of the commentary author) expedited (within two weeks) review of the commentary and recommend to the editor whether it should be published.

If the recommendation is yes, then the commentary would undergo editorial review, and the authors of the original article would be invited to write a reply to the commentary, which would also undergo editorial review. Then, both the commentary and the reply to the commentary would be published in the next available issue to ensure that the commentary is as close to the publication of the original article as possible.

DEVELOPING EXTERNAL PEER REVIEW POLICIES

The next chapter will discuss the factors that determine whether a manuscript should undergo external peer review. However, before such decisions are made, it is important to develop policies to ensure the quality of the external review process.

Duration of Review

As authors can attest, there is no universally agreed upon amount of time external peer review should take. Some journals regularly make authors wait six months or more for a decision while others operate at a faster pace. Although authors generally prefer a quick peer review process, it is more important that editors are transparent about how long authors should expect the process to take and to ensure that those self-imposed deadlines are met.

For example, one of the more prestigious journals in the field of education, *Harvard Educational Review*, uses a two-stage review process.[9] Upon submission, authors receive an email stating that their manuscript has entered the first stage of the review process, which the editors state will take approximately 12 to 16 weeks. If a manuscript makes it through the first stage of review, then authors receive an email stating that their work has entered the second stage of review, which is anticipated to take three to six months.

Collectively, then, the review process could take almost a full calendar year, which may seem excessive to most authors. However, the journal is transparent about the time required to render decisions, and authors can make an informed decision about whether to continue with the review process or pull their manuscript and submit it elsewhere.

In general, though, a year is too long to make authors wait for a publication decision. Six months is at the upper end of what is an acceptable turnaround time, and most well-run journals should be able to process manuscripts within a three-month period. Three months is the standard that we have set at *TRSE*, and as of this writing, there has not been an external review that has extended beyond 90 days. Most authors submitting to *TRSE* receive their decisions within approximately two months.

In order to ensure that the review process is completed in the desired amount of time, the various stages of the process must be divvied up accordingly. Let's assume that three months (i.e., 12 weeks) is the maximum amount of time that authors should wait for a publication decision. The initial screening of submitted manuscripts and assigning of external reviewers, then, needs to be done quickly—within, say, a week of submission. Assigning reviewers quickly allows some cushion in case reviewers are slow in accepting the invitation or they decline to review and additional selections are needed. As a general rule, the reviewers should be finalized (i.e., they have agreed to review) within two weeks of submission.

Assuming editors want to give themselves two to three weeks to assess the reviewers' comments and write the decision letter, that leaves approximately seven weeks for the reviewers to conduct their external review. There is no "magic number" of weeks that reviewers need in order to review a manuscript. The reality is that an editor could give reviewers a full year to review a manuscript, and some would write the editor on day 364 and ask for an extension. At *TRSE*, we give reviewers approximately five weeks to complete their reviews, which provides a two-week cushion to accommodate extensions or hunt down delinquent reviewers.

The bottom line is that journals quickly develop reputations based on review times. Journals that have quick review times—while still providing substantive feedback to authors—have greater author satisfaction and are more likely to receive a greater number of submissions. Therefore, it is imperative that editors establish a maximum amount of time for the external review process and do everything in their power to ensure that expectation is consistently met.

The Review Process

Anonymous review has been the subject of much debate within academic circles for decades.[10] Critics of anonymous review argue that making authors and reviewers identifiable to each other would make peer review a more collegial process and, ideally, lead to more substantive articles that benefit from productive dialogue between authors, reviewers, and editors.[11] Critics have also argued that anonymous review makes journal editors less accountable since they never have to defend their choice of reviewers. These same critics also contend that making reviewers identifiable to authors would also lessen instances of reviewers assessing manuscripts in which they have a clear conflict of interest.[12]

Anonymous review, however, remains the gold standard in academic publishing, and the vast majority of journals engage in this practice. The reason is simple; in order for reviewers to provide honest feedback to editors, they must feel confident that they will not receive retribution from authors who receive negative feedback on their work or have their manuscripts rejected.

As such, the anonymous review policy allows for the best feedback for editors to use in determining the strengths and limitations of a manuscript, which results in a journal publishing only the strongest work.[13] Certainly, anonymous review increases the potential for harsh, and sometimes unwarranted, comments by reviewers; however, editors always have the discretion of what to share with authors, a topic that will be discussed in greater depth in chapter 4.

One compromise between these two camps is the practice of publishing a list of reviewers at the end of each volume of the journal without specifically noting which manuscripts they reviewed. Publicly naming reviewers provides a modest acknowledgment of a reviewer's services, and it also provides some transparency about who editors are using to assess the work submitted to the journal.[14] It is important to note, though, that due to data protection laws passed in recent years, it is advisable to allow reviewers to opt out of having their names publicly displayed at the end of each volume.

Regardless of the journal's position on anonymous peer review, another important decision that editors must make is how many reviewers are assigned to each manuscript. The only truly correct answer to this question is "more than one." It is not fair to authors to have their work assessed by only one reviewer; moreover, it is not overly useful for editors to have to make decisions based on only one perspective.

Many journals use two reviewers per manuscript, which allows for multiple perspectives and keeps the number of reviewers needed to a minimum. However, three reviewers per manuscript is ideal because not only does it allow for more perspectives for the editor to consider, but it also provides editors with some leeway if a reviewer fails to follow through with their review assignment. If the two reviews that have been submitted are in alignment, then the editor may feel comfortable rendering a decision based on those two reviews instead of seeking an additional reviewer and delaying the process. As a general rule, more than three sets of reviews, in addition to the editor's decision letter, gets unwieldy and can overwhelm authors.

Another policy related to the review process is whether reviewers are given the opportunity to read other reviewers' comments and an anonymized version of the editor's decision letter following an editorial decision. In general, this type of sharing of information among reviewers not only provides greater editorial transparency, but it is also educative. Particularly for early-career faculty who may have not yet had much experience reviewing, being able to see how their reviews compare with other reviewers, as well as the editor's feedback to the author, can help them grow as both an author and a reviewer, which is beneficial to both the journal and the field as a whole.

At *TRSE*, we have used this sharing of reviews and decision letters to introduce the next generation of scholars to the world of academic publishing. Doctoral students can sign up to be *TRSE* reviewers, and as manuscripts are submitted that match their scholarly interests, they are assigned as a "fourth reviewer." Their review does not "count" in that it does not factor into the editor's decision on the manuscript, so it is a low-pressure assignment. The doctoral students' comments are shared with the author, who can choose to engage with them if they wish, and more importantly, at the end of the review process, the doctoral students receive copies of the other reviewers' comments, as well as the anonymized editorial decision letter.

In recent years, we have added an additional element to the program. After reading the other reviewers' comments and the editorial decision letter, the doctoral students are invited to talk about the process with one or more editorial board members who also served as reviewers on the same manuscript.[15] Based on anecdotal data and surveys of doctoral students who have taken part in this program, serving as a fourth reviewer has been instrumental in helping demystify the process of academic publishing.

Types of Decisions

The final aspect of external review that editors must determine is what types of editorial decisions will the journal render. Obviously, there has to be an "accept" option for when a manuscript is accepted without any further revisions, and there needs to be a "reject" option for when manuscripts are deemed unsuitable for the journal. However, there is quite a bit of leeway in how journals define the decisions that fall in between those two extremes, and the choice of terminology can send certain messages to authors.

Many journals use some variation of "revise/resubmit," "major revisions needed," and "minor revisions needed" to convey to authors that additional work is needed before the manuscript can be accepted for publication. These labels, however, can be confusing or misleading to authors, particularly those without extensive publishing experience.

If an author, for example, receives a "revise/resubmit" or "major revisions needed" decision, does that mean the manuscript will be accepted if the author satisfactorily completes the requested revisions? Will the revised manuscript go out for another round of external peer review? Particularly if an editor is not explicit in their decision letter, such ambiguity can be a source of stress or frustration for authors.

Therefore, it is best practice for decision labels to be as precise as possible. Editors should only use the word "accept" if they are committed to publishing the work. A decision of "accept with major revisions" should mean that, eventually, the manuscript will be published in the journal. It is an unethical practice for an editor to reject a manuscript once it has been conditionally accepted.

At *TRSE*, there are two decision categories beyond "accept" and "reject": "accept, pending revision" and "reject, encourage resubmission." If an author receives an "accept, pending revision" decision, they can be confident that the manuscript will eventually be published—although it may take multiple rounds of revisions. Manuscripts that receive this decision do not go out for additional rounds of external review; instead, the editor works with the author "in house" to get the manuscript to the point it can be deemed publishable.

TRSE uses "reject, encourage resubmission" instead of "revise/resubmit" because it is clear that the manuscript is, as currently written, not acceptable for publication. Manuscripts that receive this decision go out for another round of external review once a revision is submitted. However, by clearly rejecting the original manuscript, the author knows that publication is not guaranteed even if they attend to the reviewers' concerns.

There is, of course, an inherent danger in using "reject, encourage resubmission" instead of "revise/resubmit." It is possible that junior faculty without much publication experience or scholars not familiar with the policies of the journal may fixate on the word "reject" and not understand that this decision is actually good news. As will be discussed in chapter 4, it is exceedingly rare for manuscripts to be even conditionally accepted after the first round of external review, so a "reject, encourage resubmission" decision indicates that the manuscript has promise and is potentially publishable. Therefore, if an editor decides to use this terminology, it is important to make authors aware of its meaning.

Making the determination between "accept, pending revisions" and "reject, encourage resubmission" will be discussed in chapter 4; however, editors need to be cognizant of reviewers' time when making these decisions. Some journals will continue to send manuscripts out for external review until all of the reviewers render an "accept" decision, which is an unreasonable demand. In extreme instances, reviewers have been asked to approve punctuation and other minor errors that should be the work of copyeditors.[16]

IMPLICATIONS FOR AUTHORS

Pay Attention to What Editors Want and Know

If an editor's editorial vision aligns with the type of scholarship that one does, then it is likely worth submitting to that journal. Obviously, submitting a manuscript aligned with an editorial vision does not guarantee acceptance, but those manuscripts start with an advantage. Editing often requires making tough decisions, particularly with respect to rejecting a manuscript or giving authors a chance to revise and resubmit. Manuscripts that align with an editor's vision are likely to be given more opportunities to be successful.

Even if one is not privy to the editor's vision, the composition of the editorial team and editorial board can give clues to the types of topics and methodologies the journal values. If an author does not see their subfield or methodologies represented in either the editorial team or editorial board, then they may want to consider submitting to a different journal. It is, of course, possible to get published even if one's topic does not fit into the areas of expertise of the scholars on the editorial team or editorial board, but it may be more challenging than more "mainstream" topics.

If one's subfield is represented on the editorial team or editorial board, that is generally a good sign. However, it is important to pay attention to *who* is doing the representing since they will likely either be handling the decision-making on the manuscript (i.e., editor or associate editor) or serving as a reviewer (i.e., editorial board member).

Often academic fields have ideological fault lines on certain topics; if one aligns with one side of the debate and the member of the editorial team/board falls on the other, then they may approach the manuscript with skepticism from the outset. Even if the manuscript ideologically aligns with members of the editorial team and editorial board, it may be wise to ensure that the citations would fit the editorial team/board members' expectations (and make sure to cite their work, as appropriate!).

There is a popular misconception among authors that they have a better chance of their work getting accepted if their manuscripts fall within the editor's area of expertise. On one hand, yes, that can be beneficial; obviously, manuscripts that align with an editor's subfield are within the scope of the journal. However, editors likely will give those manuscripts a more critical read.

As will be discussed in the next chapter, the first hurdle that authors have to jump is the initial editorial review. Oftentimes editors are more likely to send manuscripts outside of their areas of expertise out for external review, even if their initial read of the manuscript is negative. When manuscripts fall within their areas of expertise, they are more confident in rendering a desk reject if they feel the manuscript is of poor quality.

Look for Advantages

Whenever possible, authors should take advantage of any initiative that narrows the pool of potential manuscripts. Special issues may create logistical headaches for editors, but they are wonderful for authors. If the topic of a special issue aligns with one's scholarship, that is an opportunity that authors do not want to miss. Moreover, special issues often operate on a specific timeline, so the editorial decision may be quicker for a special issue than what is typical for the journal.

The same theory applies for special sections of a journal. If an author has a manuscript that would fit within a certain section, it is worth contacting the section editor to see if there is potential interest in the topic. Also, in the cover letter that accompanies the manuscript at the time of submission, it is a good idea for authors to tell the editor that they would like the manuscript to be considered for a particular section of the journal.

Finally, if a journal publishes book reviews, consider reaching out to the editor (or book review editor) and volunteering to serve as a book reviewer. Oftentimes, book reviews are solicited, so it is important to get on the journal's list of reviewers. These types of publications are often easy ways to get into top-tier journals, so they are particularly useful for doctoral students and early-career faculty who want to start building reputations in their fields of study.

Determine the Journal's Reputation

Scholars, particularly those new to the field, often only look at one metric when deciding to which journal they should submit their manuscripts: acceptance rate. Certainly, acceptance rates are important to consider; a journal that has an acceptance rate of under 10% is going to have a rigorous review process. However, as will be discussed in the next chapter, acceptance rates are a little misleading because they are a reflection of all manuscripts submitted, not just the ones that go out for external review. Given that most journals receive many manuscripts that are clearly not within the scope of the journal, the "true" acceptance rate is often higher.

Therefore, the more important metric, particularly for scholars on the tenure track, is "time to decision." Increasingly, journals are posting this information on their websites, but in the event that they do not have that information readily available, it is worth talking to a mentor or a colleague about the reputation of the journal. It is also perfectly acceptable to email an editor and ask what the typical turnaround time is for manuscripts submitted to that journal (and if they fail to respond to the email, that can give an indication about the journal's responsiveness).

The time it takes to receive a decision is extremely important, particularly in the "publish or perish" atmosphere of academia. Getting rejected is part of being a scholar; it happens to everyone from time to time. It is one thing, however, to get rejected within three months; it is another to get rejected over a year after submission. What level of review time one is willing to accept will vary among individuals; if one is on the tenure track and needs a quick publication, then they should not submit to a journal with a reputation of taking longer than six months to render decisions.

Finally, one way to assess the speed of a journal's review process, as well as the level of feedback they give authors, is to volunteer to be a reviewer. Editors are always looking for new reviewers, so most will welcome unsolicited requests to review. Assuming the journal sends editorial decision letters and other reviewers' comments to reviewers at the end of the process, serving as a reviewer can be extremely informative, not only about the journal in question, but also about what constitutes quality manuscripts and reviews.

NOTES

1. Wayne Journell, "From the Editor," *Theory & Research in Social Education* 45, no. 1 (2017): 2–3. https://doi.org/10.1080/00933104.2016.1272328.

2. It is worth noting that there exist some doubts about this claim. As Arthur G. Jago found in his investigation, the claim that "as many as 50% of papers are never read by anyone other than their authors, referees, and journal editors" that was originally noted in Lokman I. Meho, "The Rise and Rise of Citation Analysis," *Physics World* 20, no. 1 (2007), 32 and subsequently repeated elsewhere (see, for example, Rose Eveleth, "Academics Write Papers Arguing Over How Many People Read (and Cite) Their Papers," *Smithsonian Magazine*, last modified March 25, 2014, https://www.smithsonianmag.com/smart-news/half-academic-studies-are-never-read-more-three-people-18095022/ and Leah Washburn-Moses, "We Make Tenure Decisions Unfairly. Here's a Better Way," *The Chronicle of Higher Education*, last modified March 27, 2018, https://www.chronicle.com/article/we-make-tenure-decisions-unfairly-heres-a-better-way/) is, at best, dubious and, at worst, completely fabricated. See Arthur G. Jago, "Can It Really Be True That Half of Academic Papers Are Never Read?," *The Chronicle of Higher Education*, last modified June 1, 2018, https://www.chronicle.com/article/can-it-really-be-true-that-half-of-academic-papers-are-never-read/. However, when looking at citation rates, it is clear that many articles do not receive as much traction as others.

3. Daniel C. Feldman, "Building and Maintaining a Strong Editorial Board and Cadre of Ad Hoc Reviewers," in *Opening the Black Box of Editorship,* ed. Yehuda

Baruch, Alison M. Konrad, Herman Aguinis, and William H. Starbuck (New York: Palgrave MacMillan, 2008), 68.

4. Feldman, "Building and Maintaining," 69.

5. Feldman, "Building and Maintaining," 72.

6. "Web of Science Journal Evaluation Process and Selection Criteria," Clarivate, accessed June 23, 2022, https://clarivate.com/products/scientific-and-academic-research/research-discovery-andworkflow-solutions/web-of-science/core-collection/editorial-selection-process/editorial-selection-process/.

7. Ram Anbazhagan, Hoglah Dasari, and Anita Yadav, "Why Publish Special Issues? An Overview of Wiley's Special Issue Program and an Editor's Experience," The Wiley Network, last modified December 16, 2019, https://www.wiley.com/network/archive/why-publish-special-issues-an-overview-of-wileys-special-issue-program-and-an-editors-experience; Rafael Repiso et al., "The Prevalence and Impact of Special Issues in Communications Journals 2015–2019," *Learned Publishing* 34, no. 4 (2021): 593–601, https://doi.org/10.1002/leap.1406; "Increasing Citations and Improving Your Impact Factor," Sage Publishing, accessed June 23, 2022, https://us.sagepub.com/en-us/nam/increasing-citations-and-improving-your-impact-factor.

8. For an extreme example of how contentious these commentaries can get, see the back-and-forth that occurred in the *Journal of Social Studies Research* between colleagues from the same university: Sarah Drake Brown, "Preparing Effective History Teachers: The Assessment Gap," *Journal of Social Studies Research* 37, no. 3 (2013): 167–77, https://doi.org/10.1016/j.jssr.2013.04.005; Gregory J. Marchant, Melinda K. Schoenfeldt, and James H. Powell, "A Response to Brown: The Role of LAMP in Content and Assessment of Teaching," *Journal of Social Studies Research* 37, no. 3 (2013): 181–82, https://doi.org/10.1016/j.jssr.2013.05.001; Sarah Drake Brown, "Response to Marchant, Schoenfeldt, and Powell," *Journal of Social Studies Research* 37, no. 3 (2013): 183–84, https://doi.org/10.1016/j.jssr.2013.05.002.

9. This information is based on my personal experience submitting manuscripts to *Harvard Educational Review*; however, their editorial policies may have changed since then.

10. Anonymous review has historically been called "blind review"; however, some have criticized that term as being ableist in nature. Thus, I am choosing to use the term "anonymous review" instead.

11. D. G. Brown, "On Doffing the Mask," *Journal of Academic Ethics* 5, no. 2–4 (2007): 217–19, https://doi.org/10.1007/s10805-007-0934-8; The Critical Social Educator Editorial Collective, "Welcome to *The Critical Social Educator*," *The Critical Social Educator* 1, no. 1 (2021): 1–5; Amber Ward et al., "Thinking with Klosterman's Razor: Diffracting 'Reviewer 2' and Research Wrongness," *Knowledge Cultures* 6, no. 2 (2018), 45.

12. Fiona Godlee, "Making Reviewers Visible: Openness, Accountability, and Credit," *Journal of the American Medical Association* 287, no. 21 (2002): 2762–65, https://doi.org/10.1001/jama.287.21.2762; Leigh Turner, "Doffing the Mask: Why Manuscript Reviewers Ought to Be Identifiable," *Journal of Academic Ethics* 1, no. 1 (2003): 41–48, https://doi.org/10.1023/A:1025454331738; Leigh Turner, "Promoting

F.A.I.T.H in Peer Review: Five Core Attributes of Effective Peer Review," *Journal of Academic Ethics* 1, no. 2 (2003): 181–88, https://doi.org/10.1023/B:JAET .0000006844.09724.98.

13. J. Angelo Corlett, "Ethical Issues in Journal Peer-Review," *Journal of Academic Ethics* 2, no. 4 (2005): 355–66. https://doi.org/10.1007/s10805-005-9001-1; J. Angelo Corlett, "The Ethics of Academic Journal Editing," *Journal of Academic Ethics* 6, no. 3 (2008): 205–9, https://doi.org/10.1007/s10805-008-9067-7.

14. Corlett, "Ethical Issues," 362; Turner, "Doffing the Mask," 46; Turner, "Promoting F.A.I.T.H.," 184–85.

15. In the event that the doctoral student reviewed a manuscript that was not reviewed by any members of the editorial board, I offer to debrief the review process with them.

16. I have personally experienced this type of excessive peer review. A journal that shall remain nameless once sent one of my manuscripts out for four rounds of external review; the last round consisted of reviewers approving a semicolon instead of a comma and a word choice recommended in the previous round of review.

Chapter 3

To Review or Not to Review

Desk Rejects and Assigning Reviewers

The editorial decisions that receive the most attention are the ones that editors make after external review, which is the subject of the next chapter. Yet those decisions are made in concert with recommendations made by reviewers, which provides some limits to an editor's oversight. Editors actually have the greatest unilateral control when manuscripts are first submitted—determining whether a manuscript qualifies for external review and, if so, who should review it.

DESK REJECTS

Editors are the first people to screen manuscripts after they are submitted to a journal, and they make the important decision of whether to send the manuscript out for external review or end the review process at that point through a desk reject. This decision often relies solely on the editor's discretion, although they may choose to solicit advice from other members of the editorial team, as needed. As such, editors wield a great deal of power at this stage of the review process.

A natural question to ask is why editors should desk reject manuscripts at all. Certainly, it would be more democratic to have all manuscripts submitted to a journal sent out for external review. Desk rejects, however, serve an important function: they prevent journals from overworking reviewers. Reviewers' time is precious, and they participate in external review without compensation, so it is essential that editors do not have them waste their time commenting on manuscripts that are clearly not a good fit for the journal. In fact, many reviewers will stop agreeing to review manuscripts for a journal if they are sent too many substandard manuscripts that, in their opinion, should have been desk rejected.

There are two primary criteria for desk rejecting a manuscript. The first is lack of fit. All journals, but particularly top-tier journals, international journals, and indexed journals with impact factors, will receive submissions that are clearly not within the scope of the journal. Oftentimes, these manuscripts can be spotted from the title alone. For example, *TRSE*, a journal focusing on social studies education, has received manuscripts on topics ranging from mathematics and computer science to nursing.

Other times, the lack of fit requires a bit more reading. Particularly if a journal is focused on a certain aspect of a field, it is not unusual for it to receive manuscripts that are close in scope but still not suitable for the journal. For example, the *Journal of Teacher Education* is a journal that focuses, as the name would suggest, on research related specifically to teacher education. Annually, they receive a large number of submissions that pertain to K–12 teaching or education broadly, but they are desk rejected because they do not speak directly to teacher education. In many cases, these manuscripts are well-written and are illustrative of methodologically solid research; however, they do not fit the scope of the journal.[1]

Although these types of inappropriate submissions can be annoying, they do not require much time to process. Editors should develop some boilerplate language that they can quickly send to authors. For example, the typical desk reject letter that I send authors whose work does not fit the scope of *TRSE* is:

> Dear [Author],
> Thank you for your submission to *Theory & Research in Social Education* entitled, "[Title of Article]." I have had the opportunity to read your manuscript, and I am afraid that it would not fare well under external review. Therefore, I have decided not to send it out for review for the following reasons:
>
> - It is beyond the scope of the journal. Articles published in *TRSE* must show a clear connection between concepts and the teaching of history/ social studies education or civic education.
>
> I understand that the decision not to send your manuscript out for review is disappointing, but hopefully this will allow you to find a more suitable outlet for your work more quickly. I hope this decision will not deter you from submitting manuscripts to *TRSE* in the future.

It often shocks authors to find out that desk rejects due to lack of fit are exceedingly common. Many journals desk reject upwards of 40% of all submissions that they receive! The reasons for these types of clearly inappropriate submissions are hard to pinpoint.

Occasionally, as with the example from the *Journal of Teacher Education* given above, the submissions are well intentioned and likely made by novice scholars who may not know the reputation of the journals in their field. The vast majority of desk rejects of inappropriate manuscripts, however, often have no rhyme or reason. It is possible that in some countries or at some universities, scholars get "credit" for having work under review; therefore, they simply send their work to top-tier journals so that they can put "manuscript under review" on their annual reviews.

The more challenging desk rejects are the ones that fall into the second criterion for deciding not to send a manuscript out for external review, which is when the manuscript has a "fatal flaw" that would keep it from being published. Oftentimes, the fatal flaw is methodological, but occasionally, it could be that the study is not properly contextualized with relevant literature or that the findings simply replicate what is already widely known within the field. In any case, this type of desk reject means that the editor has determined that the manuscript is not worth sending to reviewers because it would ultimately lead to a reject decision.

This type of desk reject is certainly more subjective, and a general guideline is that if an editor is having a hard time deciding whether a fatal flaw exists, they should send the manuscript out for review. This type of desk reject letter follows the same format as the aforementioned example, except that the editor should provide a detailed explanation of the fatal flaw that prevented the manuscript from being sent out for external review. If appropriate, editors can offer alternative outlets for the author to consider (e.g., if there is a methodological issue, perhaps they could rework the manuscript into a practitioner piece).

On rare occasions, it may be advisable for editors to bend the rules a bit. If a manuscript fits the scope of the journal, focuses on an interesting topic, and is methodologically sound but has a fatal, but potentially fixable, flaw, editors can desk reject the manuscript but give the author an opportunity to revise the manuscript and resubmit it as a new manuscript that would then undergo external review. Although some authors may bristle at being asked to revise their manuscript before peer review, fixing obvious limitations at the outset greatly improves their chances for success later on.

Finally, a decision to desk reject a manuscript should be made quickly. It is unethical for editors to hold onto a manuscript for weeks only to reject it with minimal feedback given to the author. Barring unforeseen circumstances, desk rejects should be rendered within days of initial submission. Doing so not only keeps them from piling up, but it also allows authors to quickly find a more appropriate outlet for their work.

SELECTING REVIEWERS

It is necessary to preface this section by acknowledging two truths about academic publishing. First, reviewing for journals is unpaid—and often unacknowledged—labor. Reviewing is a service to the field that may not be valued by one's university in terms of annual reviews, merit raises, or promotion and tenure decisions. It is easy to become frustrated with unresponsive or delinquent reviewers, but editors should always be mindful that completing reviews is rarely at the top of reviewers' priority lists.

The second truth is that anonymous reviewing is not truly anonymous. Although the reviewers and the authors do not know each other's identities, the editor knows the identity of both. The selection of reviewers is perhaps the most important factor in determining whether a manuscript is ultimately accepted. Therefore, the selection of reviewers is extremely important and should not be made lightly or carelessly.

The Mechanics of the External Review Process

Academic publishing has evolved considerably from the days when authors had to mail hard copies of manuscripts to editors, who then had to forward them via the postal service to reviewers. Today, most major journals are housed within large publishing companies (e.g., Taylor & Francis, Sage, Elsevier), and all correspondence between editors and reviewers occurs via publication management systems that create emails with prewritten templates at the click of a button. These publication management systems can also be programmed to send reminder emails to both reviewers and authors, as well as notifications to editors when all reviews for a manuscript have been submitted.

In many ways, then, the process of dealing with reviewers has been automated. However, that does not mean editors can simply select reviewers and forget about them. Ensuring that external review times remain within the range that the editor deems acceptable requires a near-daily monitoring of the publication management system. A quick scan can identify manuscripts that do not have sufficient reviewers or have reviewers who have missed their deadlines, which requires action by the editor.

The initial email inviting a reviewer to assess a manuscript is pretty standard. Editors should include the title of the manuscript and the abstract to give the potential reviewer some context about whether the request falls within their area of expertise (as well as if they may have a conflict of interest to which the editor was unaware). Perhaps the most important information to include is the *exact date* when the review is due. Some journals use vague language, such as "four weeks from now" or "around a month," which is just begging for delinquent reviews. To give an example, here is the script used for initial reviewer requests at *TRSE*:

Dear [Name of Potential Reviewer]:
  A manuscript has been submitted for possible publication in *Theory & Research in Social Education* for which I think you would be an excellent reviewer. The article is entitled [Name of Article]. The abstract appears at the end of this letter. I would be grateful if you would kindly agree to act as a reviewer for this paper. If you are able to review the manuscript, I would like to receive your comments no later than [Due Date].
  Please let me know as soon as possible if you will be able to accept my invitation to review. To do this, please click the appropriate link below to automatically register your reply with our online manuscript submission and review system, or e-mail me with your reply.
  *** PLEASE NOTE: This is a two-step process. After clicking on the link, you will be directed to a web page to confirm. ***
  [Links for Accept Request, Decline Request, and Unavailable]
  Should you accept my invitation to review this manuscript, you will be sent an email with a direct link to the score sheet, which will be made available to you. You will then have access to the manuscript and reviewer instructions in your Reviewer Center.
  If you are unable to review the manuscript, click on the "decline" option to register your response. This will direct you to a screen where you will be given the opportunity to provide details of any alternative reviewers. Your suggestions will be much appreciated.
  [Manuscript Abstract]

The only time to vary this initial message is when editors are asking potential reviewers to review a manuscript that has been revised and resubmitted. Whenever possible, it is advisable to send a revised manuscript to the same reviewers who reviewed the original iteration of the manuscript, particularly if they recommended that the manuscript be revised and resubmitted. Doing so gives the author the best chance for acceptance. If a reviewer recommended "reject," and it is clear that they have an irreconcilable ideological issue with the work, then it is not fair to the author to send the revision to that reviewer.

It is, therefore, important for editors to keep track of when forthcoming resubmissions are due and which reviewers will be assigned to the revision when it is submitted. If not, then it is easy to inadvertently assign a new submission to those reviewers in the interim, which would prevent them from reviewing the revision when it is submitted (or require the editor to beg a reviewer to complete multiple reviews simultaneously!). When assigning manuscripts to an associate editor, is also important to let them know which reviewers are "off the table" for consideration due to the likelihood they will be called on to review a forthcoming resubmission.

When being asked to review a resubmission, reviewers appreciate being given an anonymized copy of the original decision letter and the anonymized cover letter that authors submit along with the manuscript that details how they responded to the reviewers' and editor's suggestions from the first round of external review. Therefore, it is necessary to change the body of the invitation accordingly. Here is an example from *TRSE* for an email to a potential reviewer who also served as a reviewer during the first round of external review:

> Dear [Name of Potential Reviewer]
> A while back, you reviewed the original version of the above manuscript for *TRSE* that was given a "reject, encourage resubmission" decision from the journal (your recommendation was "[Their Publication Recommendation From First Round of Review]"). The author(s) have submitted a revised manuscript, and given your familiarity with the original manuscript, I would appreciate if you would also serve as a reviewer for the revision.
> The abstract appears at the end of this letter, and I have also attached the following items that may help you with your evaluation of the manuscript:
>
> - a blinded copy of my original decision letter
> - a blinded copy of the author's response to the reviewers' feedback
>
> If you are able to review the manuscript, I would like to receive your comments no later than [Due Date].

In the event that the revised submission is sent to a reviewer who did not serve as a reviewer during the first round of external review, the first paragraph of that email is changed to:

> For your information, the above manuscript is a revision of a manuscript that was given a "reject encourage resubmission" decision from the journal. The author(s) have submitted a revised manuscript, and given your scholarly expertise, I would appreciate if you would serve as a reviewer for the revision.

Of utmost importance is maintaining the integrity of the anonymous review process. When authors submit a manuscript, as well as a letter detailing how they have revised their manuscript in response to reviewer feedback in the case of a revised submission, it is essential that neither contains the author's name or includes other identifying information (e.g., is written on university letterhead). Although authors should anonymize manuscripts/letters on their own, occasionally they forget. One place that authors often overlook, for example, is the "properties" section of Microsoft Word. When mistakes happen, editors can either manually anonymize the manuscripts themselves or send them back to the author.

In an ideal world, once reviewers receive the request, they quickly accept, and the external review process starts. Of course, some reviewers decline the request, and when they do, the editor must assign a different potential reviewer to take their place. By far, the most frustrating aspect of assigning reviewers is "request purgatory," or when reviewers neither accept nor decline the reviewer request. When the request just sits in potential reviewers' inboxes, it stalls the entire process; editors do not know if they should select additional reviewers or wait and see if the selected reviewer comes through.

A good rule of thumb is to wait three to four work days to see if a reviewer responds to the request. At that point, it is worth sending reminders. I typically send a passive-aggressive email from my university account at the three-day mark that says

> I hope you are doing well. A few days ago, I sent you a reviewer request for *TRSE*, but I have not heard back from you yet. I know those automated emails sometimes end up in spam folders, so I am following up with a personal email. If you could please accept or decline the request soon, I would appreciate it. If you need me to resend the request, please let me know.

Occasionally, the emails from the publication management system actually do get sent to spam folders, so the personal email can assist in those cases. More likely, the personal email is not as easily ignored as the automated email, so it usually prompts the reviewer to either accept or decline the request. Of course, sometimes it does not work, and then I usually have the publication management system send another automated email at the seven-day mark. At that point, if the reviewer has not responded, I move forward with selecting a different potential reviewer.

In those cases, editors can choose to let the original reviewer know that they are no longer needed or let the request sit in their inboxes. If they do the latter, on rare occasions, the originally selected reviewer will agree to do the review two or three weeks after the request was sent. At that point, editors can decide whether the additional feedback would be useful or if the reviewer can be excused from the assignment.

Once all reviewers have agreed, then the manuscript goes into a holding pattern until the reviews are due. During this time, it is useful to have reminder emails automatically sent from the publication management system, usually around one week before the review is due and, if the review is tardy, a few days after the due date.

Some reviewers will be proactive and email the editor, letting them know that the review will be a few days late. Other reviewers will let the deadline pass, and it is incumbent on the editor to reach out about the status of the review. If the automated reminders do not do the trick, then a personal email is appropriate. I usually send something short and sweet along the lines of "I hope you are doing well. According to [the publication management system], you had a review due a couple of days ago. Could you please give me an update on when I should expect to receive it?"

Most reviewers eventually get their reviews submitted, even if it is several days late. On occasion, however, the repeated reminders are not enough, and editors must decide when to either seek an additional reviewer, which may extend the external review process by several weeks, or make an editorial decision based on the reviews that have already been submitted. There is no set time frame to make this decision; however, if it has been two weeks from the due date and the reviewer has not responded to any of the reminders, it is unlikely that they will complete the review.

Considerations for Selecting Reviewers

The selection of reviewers can greatly affect the eventual outcome of the review process. As a general rule, editors should choose reviewers that give authors the best chance of being accepted. That stance does not mean that editors should send manuscripts to authors' friends or known "easy" reviewers (see next chapter); doing so would be unethical. In this case, giving authors the "best chance" means not knowingly sending their work to reviewers who would have strong ideological or methodological objections to it.

Most academic fields have ideological schisms that are irreconcilable. For example, in social studies education, there is much debate over the concept of historical empathy. Some scholars see historical empathy as a primarily cognitive endeavor, whereas others believe there is an affective aspect involved in students' understanding of the past.[2]

If a manuscript on historical empathy that employs a cognitive framework is submitted to *TRSE*, the chances of it being accepted diminish considerably if it is sent to reviewers who are in the affective camp, and vice versa. That is not to say that editors cannot send manuscripts to reviewers who have a range of perspectives, but it is important to keep those ideological camps in mind when rendering a decision.

The same logic applies to methodology. There is nothing wrong with sending a manuscript to a reviewer who is not an expert in the methodology used in the article; they can comment on other aspects of the manuscript that do fall within their area of expertise. However, as methodological boundaries are pushed within fields, some traditionalists take the stance that the new methods are not rigorous or lack validity. Sending a manuscript with an innovative methodological approach to such a reviewer will almost surely result in a "reject" recommendation, no matter any other strengths of the manuscript.

A less discussed source of potential bias among reviewers can be found in manuscripts that focus on race, gender, sexuality, or other aspects of identity. Although it is certainly possible for, say, White scholars to review manuscripts focusing on race, it is important for editors to acknowledge potential biases and limitations related to their lived experiences that White scholars might bring to their evaluation of such manuscripts. To illustrate this point, here is a Twitter thread published in in early 2022 by Chezare Warren, a scholar at Vanderbilt University, that shared a letter he wrote to an editor of an academic journal following the rejection of a manuscript[3]:

> First, let me say [because of my editorial experience] . . . I am clear about how much work and thought goes into a decision. This work is not easy, and I want to both acknowledge and honor the effort you both exert to carry out your duties with integrity and excellence. Thank you! My coauthors and I do believe that the reviews are helpful in moving the paper forward. That said, we are concerned about the fairness of the decision made, and what this decision communicates about the type of work [journal name redacted] values.
>
> The first reviewer is in clear support of the paper. Similarly, the third reviewer is supportive while also offering copious feedback that is fairly cosmetic. By cosmetic I mean, much of this individual's review urged us to add more examples, reorganize the text for clarity, or simply be more explicit about our thinking. These are revisions that could be easily addressed. Both reviewer 1 and reviewer 3 led with the importance of our study for advancing discourse about Black boys in education, and the paper's novelty, which is a hallmark for scholarship published in [journal name redacted]. Neither of these two reviewers offer feedback about the validity of our findings and claims, or question with much vigor at all the rigor of our methodological approach. This leads my coauthors and I to perceive that your decision as editors may be most informed by feedback from reviewer two, whose comments we believe are compromised because of her admission to being offended as a white woman with the study itself.
>
> It is clear from our reading of the feedback that reviewer 2 wanted us to write an altogether different paper. Rather than substantively engage with the logic, argument, and claims we did make, she centered herself and her desires—a white researcher who has "interviewed a lot of teachers on the topic of teacher-student relationships," a former teacher, and a white woman admittedly struggling with her inability to "escape" the "omnipresence" of racism. Reviewer 2 insists that we focus on a local school setting, and avoid the societal context in our analyses. This misses the larger point of the paper. Our study purposefully centers the voices of young Black men and boys, and in doing so, our analyses make an

explicit connection between their experiences of interactions with educators in school to broader social constructions of the ways Black bodies tend to be read, seen, known, and understood following 250+ years of enslavement and 350+ years of Black people's abject racial oppression in the U.S.

Naming antiblackness as a residual consequence of slavery and its association with the ways that educators choose to interact with Black boys is essential to nuancing what we know about establishing and sustaining positive student-adult relationships with Black people, let alone [Black] boys. Again, because of the substantive focus on Black boys' experience of school—and our framing of connection as a prerequisite to the types of relationships that can make P-20 schools more humanizing places for Black boys—we use the literature review in our paper to demonstrate how American schools are sites of pain and suffering, which reviewer 2 disagreed with, imploring us to offer more connection to the literature on "student-teacher relationships" (read: literature primarily written by white people that does not take a critical, race-centric approach in its design or analyses), and we do cite prominent scholars in this area at various points throughout the paper . . .

Finally, reviewer 2 laments, "I know the deep affection and high hopes teachers cherish for their students," as if to suggest that our paper does not also acknowledge teachers' good intentions . . . But, what is especially troubling, is that it is clear reviewer 2 has made her recommendations about the quality of the paper through the lens of her frustration. She feels antagonized, and as a result, raises numerous concerns about the claims and validity of our findings without ever having to really contend with the substance of our arguments. As we state explicitly in the paper at the beginning of the methods section, "Epistemologically speaking, our stance as researchers maintains that antiblackness is each American's inheritance, the result of slavery. As such antiblackness is an omnipresent force always shading how Black boys are seen, known, and understood in the world—inside and outside of school." . . . It is fine to disagree with that stance, but we find that reviewer 2 does not offer us a compelling reason why, other than that the study "made [her] defensive" and that as a "white female" she is discombobulated by having to query of herself "are all my comments towards students of different skin color racist (even if I mean them well)?" In sum, the entire review is disconcerting, and leads my coauthors and I to believe reviewer 2's implicit racial bias shades the feedback she offered, clouded her scholarly judgment, and therefore renders her review unreliable.

We are asking that the editorial team reconsider outright rejecting the paper, and allow my coauthors and I the opportunity to resubmit a revised paper for another round of review. We recognize that it is well within your right to deny this request, which would of course be disappointing. I do believe, however, that as editors you want to do what is best for the journal; that you value diverse viewpoints and experiences, and would rather avoid (the appearance of) reinforcing racial bias that justice-oriented scholarship like this is too often subject to . . .

As Warren's letter illustrates, it is important for editors to seek diverse reviewers, particularly when dealing with manuscripts focusing on topics related to Black, Indigenous, and People of Color (BIPOC) communities. Doing so can have profound effects on the type of scholarship published in a journal.

To illustrate, Appendix A lists all of the manuscripts submitted to *TRSE* between July 1, 2016 and December 31, 2021 that focused on race and were sent out for external review; the demographics of the reviewers assigned to those manuscripts; and the publication recommendations made by those reviewers. Eighty percent of those manuscripts had at least one reviewer who was a Scholar of Color, and 45% had two or more Scholars of Color who served as reviewers. It is likely not a coincidence that 50% of these manuscripts were eventually accepted, which is well above the overall 10% acceptance rate of the journal.

Appendix A also shows that having BIPOC reviewers does not guarantee that manuscripts focusing on race or critical topics will be accepted. It does not take long scrolling through academic spaces on social media to see critical scholars complaining that their manuscripts were rejected simply because editors and/or reviewers did not understand or appreciate their work. As Warren's letter shows, such ignorance on the part of reviewers can happen; however, reviewer bias is far from the only reason why critical manuscripts get rejected.

An illustrative example can be found in manuscript UTRS-2016–0087 (see Appendix A). That manuscript focused on the field of social studies education's failure to adequately address race within its scholarly communities. Given the topic, I knew it would be controversial, so I sent it to four reviewers in order to receive a variety of perspectives. As Appendix A shows, three of the four reviewers were BIPOC scholars, and two of them recommended the manuscript be rejected, along with a White scholar.

However, the one BIPOC scholar who recommended that the manuscript be accepted disclosed in her comments to the author that she was a Black woman. When I rendered the "reject" decision to the author, they sent me a polite, but accusatory email asserting that I had not valued the perspective of the Black woman reviewer when making my decision, with the implication being that the other reviewers were White and that I had relied on their opinions instead.

I responded to the author by letting them know that three of the reviewers were Scholars of Color and that all four reviewers took critical perspectives to their work. In other words, the issue was not that the reviewers were not ideologically aligned with the focus of the manuscript; rather, the manuscript had serious flaws that the reviewers believed could not be remedied via revision.

In short, manuscripts should be evaluated on the basis of what they are, as opposed to what they are not or what reviewers think they should have been. It is essential that editors utilize reviewers who can offer fair reads of manuscripts and offer critiques that are not based on ideological or methodological disagreements beyond the author's control. Doing so not only provides authors with the best chance for success, but it also can help a journal diversify the scholarship found within its pages.

IMPLICATIONS FOR AUTHORS

Understanding Desk Rejects

One of the most challenging aspects of academic publishing is deciding to which journal one should send their work. The number of scholarly journals has increased significantly over the past few decades, and while having choices is generally positive, it makes finding the right fit for a manuscript more difficult. Understanding desk rejects can help authors better navigate this dilemma.

Scholars often base their decision on acceptance rates. If they feel as though they have an exceptional manuscript, they will submit to a more exclusive journal with a low acceptance rate. If they think the manuscript is just a solid piece of scholarship, they may defer to a midtier journal with a seemingly more reasonable acceptance rate. Overall, this logic is sound; top-tier journals tend to be more selective, and they publish high-quality work.

However, many scholars, particularly scholars on the tenure track who are in "publish or perish" mode, may be selling their solid manuscripts a bit short if they just focus on acceptance rates. Given that most journals desk reject a significant number of submissions and that top-tier journals attract more overall submissions than most midtier journals, thus leading to even more desk rejects, it is likely that the acceptance rates between top-tier and midtier journals are closer than most authors think. Therefore, assuming all other factors (e.g., external review time) are equal, it may be worth submitting to the top-tier journal and seeing what happens.

Receiving desk rejects can also be educative. All scholars receive desk rejects on occasion; however, if one is receiving a steady number of desk rejects, it means that either their work is problematic or, more likely, they need to become better read within their field of study. Ensuring that one's manuscript fits the scope of a journal—both ideologically and methodologically—is essential to both getting published and not wasting time on the tenure track.

The only way to truly get a sense of a journal's scope is to read it consistently. Some journals are clearly empirical in scope, and others are clearly aimed at practitioners. However, some journals allow for both, but they often have a certain hybrid style to them. When reading journals, do not just focus on articles of interest; even articles that fall outside of one's specific research area can provide important information about the kinds of methodologies and perspectives the journal values.

It is important not to take desk rejects personally. Editors render them out of compassion for both reviewers' *and* authors' time. While finding out that one's manuscript is not a good fit for a journal is never pleasant, receiving that information in a matter of days is certainly preferable to waiting several months and receiving a clear-cut "reject" decision. Finally, if an editor renders a desk reject but offers the author the opportunity to make changes and resubmit, it is wise to do so. The editor is acknowledging that the overall topic is of interest to the journal.

Recognizing Potential Biases

Ensuring that a manuscript falls within the scope of a journal is the baseline criterion for considering whether to submit one's work there. Many manuscripts might technically fall within the scope of a journal—and, thus, would not receive a desk reject—but, in reality, have little chance of being published due to unofficial ideological or methodological biases held by either the editor or the reviewers that they use. Not recognizing these implicit biases may actually be more harmful than simply misreading the scope of a journal due to the amount of time the external review process takes.

It is always wise to take note on who is being published in the journal, as well as the ideological stances that the journal allows. Do Scholars of Color regularly publish in the journal? Does the journal allow for critical perspectives that push the status quo, or is it fairly traditional in the types of research it publishes? Does the journal publish studies that use a variety of methodologies? If the answer to those questions is no, it may be a signal that the journal is not welcoming to diverse perspectives, regardless of what it states in the "aims and scope" description on the journal website.

Talking with mentors can help authors navigate these "unofficial" questions of fit. It is also important to acknowledge that journals can evolve over time, often aligned with changing trends in the field, broadly speaking. Also, new editorial teams often introduce new priorities, as well as a different pool of reviewers, which can drastically alter the type of content published within the journal's pages.

Understanding the External Review Process

All authors get impatient with slow external review processes, and sometimes rightfully so. There are, however, a lot of moving parts within the external review process, and only a couple of them are under the control of the editor. Therefore, before authors take out their ire on an editor, it is worth remembering that the delay is likely due to a delinquent reviewer.

Two dilemmas that authors face are when to contact an editor for a status update and when to pull a manuscript from publication consideration due to an overly long external review process. In some ways, these two questions are linked. One should never badger an editor before three months have passed, and it may be more effective if authors wait until the six-month mark to send a politely worded email asking when one should expect to receive a decision. Ideally, the editor responds by providing the author with an updated time frame.

If the editor is unresponsive, then authors face a difficult decision. Pulling a manuscript should be considered a last resort. If an author pulls a manuscript, then they will have to start the process over with a new journal, which could potentially double the amount of time the manuscript spends under review. Yet, it may not be worth leaving the manuscript under review with a journal indefinitely. Ultimately, this decision must be weighed against the following factors:

- Whether the author is on the tenure track (i.e., how fast do they need this decision?)
- The author's publication record (i.e., do they really need this publication to make a case for promotion and/or tenure?)
- The prestige of the journal (i.e., if it is a strong study, it might be the best chance an author has to get into the top journal in their field, so it is worth the wait)
- The likelihood of acceptance (i.e., if it was an aspirational journal, then it makes more sense to pull the manuscript than if the journal is likely to accept the work)
- How much frustration the author is willing to endure

In short, there is not a clear answer. As a general rule of thumb, though, if one has not received a decision within eight months of submission, and the editor has not provided a status update, it is worth seriously considering pulling the manuscript.

NOTES

1. Kenneth T. Henson, "Writing for Publication: A Shift in Perspective," *Phi Delta Kappan* 90, no. 10 (2009): 776c, https://doi.org/10.1177%2F003172170909001023.

2. Examples of the cognitive approach are Tim Huijgen et al., "Toward Historical Perspective Taking: Students' Reasoning When Contextualizing the Actions of People in the Past," *Theory & Research in Social Education* 45, no. 1 (2017): 110–41, https://doi.org/10.1080/00933104.2016.1208597 and Peter Sexias and Tom Morton, *The Big Six: Historical Thinking Concepts* (Toronto: Nelson, 2013). Examples of the affective approach include Keith C. Barton and Linda S. Levstik, *Teaching History for the Common Good* (Mahwah: Lawrence Erlbaum Associates, 2004) and Jason Endacott and Sarah Brooks, "An Updated Theoretical and Practical Model for Promoting Historical Empathy," *Social Studies Research and Practice* 8, no. 1 (2013): 41–58.

3. Chezare A. Warren (@chezareaugustus), "Just because the editor(s) don't get it, doesn't mean the work is not good or that it lacks value #Selah," Tweet, January 5, 2022, https://twitter.com/chezareaugustus/status/1478888976224178177. It is worth noting that Warren and his colleagues eventually got their study published—six years after the rejection that prompted this letter: Chezare A. Warren, Dorinda J. Carter Andrews, and Terry K. Flennaugh, "Connection, Antiblackness, and Positive Relationships That (Re)Humanize Black Boys' Experience of School," *Teachers College Record* 124, no. 1 (2022): 111–42, https://doi.org/10.1177%2F01614681221086115.

Chapter 4

The Buck Stops Here

Making Editorial Decisions

Once the reviews come in, the fate of the manuscript lies squarely with the editor. In a perfect world, all the reviews for a manuscript would come back either "accept" or "reject," but it is rarely that straightforward. If an editor has done a good job of weeding out clearly unacceptable manuscripts at the desk reject stage, it is rare for all of the reviewers to recommend a manuscript be flat-out rejected. Rarer still is having all of the reviewers recommend "accept with revision" on the first round of external review.[1] Occasionally, all three reviewers will recommend that a manuscript be revised and resubmitted, but even that is unusual.

More often than not, one reviewer will recommend the manuscript be rejected, another will recommend "accept with revisions," and the third will recommend that the author be given the opportunity to revise and resubmit without a guarantee of acceptance. In those cases, it is tempting to just "average" the recommendations and give the author a "reject, encourage resubmission" decision.

However, there are a host of reasons why the decision-making process should not be that simple.[2] Arriving at an editorial decision and conveying to authors what exactly that decision means involves a great deal of thought and precision. This chapter explores the complexity of making editorial decisions and offers tips for writing detailed and constructive decision letters.

PRACTICAL CONSIDERATIONS

At the outset, it is important to note two practical issues that editors must consider when determining the fate of manuscripts. The first is ensuring enough articles in each issue/volume. Reviewers are often better at rejecting manuscripts than accepting them, and as Alison Konrad, former editor of

Group & Organization Management, noted, it is an editor's responsibility to ensure that manuscripts are not held "to an impossible standard of perfection."[3] Reviewers also evaluate manuscripts in isolation. An editor must evaluate manuscripts within the context of the overall health of a journal. If the number of accepted articles drops too low, it can lead to negative ramifications for the journal.

For example, the current rules for inclusion in the Web of Science and impact factor eligibility state that journals must publish enough articles to "demonstrate [that] the journal is attracting sufficient interest from the relevant scholarly community to be sustainable."[4] While that definition does not mandate a specific number of articles per volume, unofficially, 20 articles per volume is considered the minimum number to demonstrate sufficient interest.

For a quarterly journal like *TRSE*, that means, on average, five articles per issue. At first glance, such a requirement may not seem too onerous. If a journal receives around 200 submissions per year and has a 10% acceptance rate, then they would be right on the mark. The more submissions a journal receives, the more selective they can be. If overall submissions—or more specifically, quality submissions—declines, then they may have to adapt by accepting more manuscripts.

As a disciplinary journal, *TRSE* does not receive as many submissions as a generalist journal might. In recent years, however, there had been a steady increase in the number of submissions per year:

- 2018: 138 submissions
- 2019: 167 submissions
- 2020: 211 submissions

At the outset of the COVID-19 pandemic, I had worried that the pandemic would result in a significant drop in submissions due to authors having to homeschool kids, not being able to collect data in schools, and experiencing general stress. However, the exact opposite happened; many scholars must have made good use of their 2020 quarantine because the journal received a record number of submissions that year.

The slowdown did occur, though, just a year later than predicted. In 2021, *TRSE* only received 188 submissions—still higher than 2018 and 2019, but short of what had occurred in 2020. More importantly, the number of *quality* submissions (i.e., submissions good enough to send out for external review) declined considerably in 2021. Compounding the problem further, there was an unusually high number of authors receiving invitations to revise and resubmit their manuscripts who either did not do so or needed lengthy extensions, likely due to time constraints created by the pandemic.

The slow pace of academic publishing often delays the effects of decreased submissions. The increased number of submissions in 2020 provided enough of a backlog of accepted manuscripts that publishing 20 articles in 2021 was never a concern. However, as the calendar turned to the first issues of the 2022 volume, the shortfall of quality submissions and lack of resubmitted manuscripts in 2021 began to emerge as a potential problem.

Even if submissions picked up in 2022, it would not immediately address the issue due to the other practical consideration that editors must always keep in the back of their minds: time. A quarterly journal is published in established intervals throughout the year; *TRSE* issues, for example, are published in March, June, September, and December. However, the publisher requests accepted manuscripts for each issue well in advance. For example, for the March 2022 issue, Taylor & Francis requested the full table of contents by January 11, 2022.

This issue of time is compounded by the fact that the process from submission to acceptance is painfully slow. As discussed in the previous chapter, when a manuscript is submitted to *TRSE,* three reviewers are usually secured within a week. Then, reviewers have approximately five weeks to submit their feedback (and that assumes that none of them are tardy or ask for extensions).

If the decision is a "reject, encourage resubmission," the authors have three months to complete the revisions. The revised manuscript goes back out for another round of external review for five weeks, and hopefully the decision is then "accept with revisions." Even then, the authors still need approximately a month to complete the requested revisions.

Unfortunately, little can be done to expedite this process. When there is concern about a potential shortage of accepted manuscripts, it is good to keep this timeline in mind. If an editor is between a "reject, encourage resubmission" and an "accept with revisions" decision, it may make sense to go ahead and give the latter decision because it guarantees the manuscript will be accepted (i.e., very little chance the author will not submit a revision), and the amount of time given to complete the revisions is shorter. Similarly, an editor with a potential dearth of accepted manuscripts may choose to give an author a chance to revise and resubmit when they might normally render a reject decision.

Is it ideal to make determinations about manuscripts based on these practical concerns? No, but an editor does a disservice to their journal if they do not keep them in mind. Editors should never abandon standards of quality, but at the same time it is impossible to completely dismiss the demands of publishers, industry requirements, and external conditions that may influence the number of quality submissions a journal receives. The rest of this chapter, however, will approach the decision-making process under the assumption that the number of quality submissions and accepted manuscripts is not a concern.

AN ANALOGY

One reason why the decision-making process is not straightforward is that reviewers are not consistent. Even when given guidelines on how to assess manuscripts, most reviewers take a holistic approach, and they often differ in what they perceive to be important. Some reviewers, for example, may assess a manuscript mainly on technical aspects (i.e., is it a methodologically rigorous, well-theorized study?); other reviewers may only recommend accepting a manuscript if they feel it makes a significant contribution to the field, even if the study is sound. In short, there is a fair amount of subjectivity that comes into play, and some reviewers have higher standards than others.

A sports analogy is useful to help make sense of the inconsistencies found in reviewers' publication recommendations. There are few topics that elicit as much passion among sports fans as which players deserve to be enshrined in their respective halls of fame. Many pints of beer have been shared among friends while arguing the cases for their favorite players and making statements such as "if Player X is in, then how can they keep Player Y out?"

The hall of fame that has the most history and, arguably, the highest standards is that of Major League Baseball, which is housed in Cooperstown, New York. Although there are technical requirements that all players must meet to be eligible for consideration (e.g., must play at least 10 years in the major leagues), the criteria for election are rather vague: "voting shall be based upon the player's record, playing ability, integrity, sportsmanship, character, and contributions to the team(s) on which the player played."[5] In reality, the only real criterion is that a player has to be listed on at least 75% of ballots cast by the Baseball Writers' Association of America (BBWAA).

Over the years, the BBWAA has been shown to be a fickle group that contains an array of opinions on what constitutes a hall of famer. Just as an editor can easily desk reject a manuscript that is clearly not appropriate for a journal, the BBWAA does not seriously entertain the cases of players who no baseball fan would ever argue deserves a place in the Hall of Fame. Thus, players like Mario Mendoza, a shortstop whose hitting futility led to a .200 batting average being colloquially described as the "Mendoza line" in baseball circles, either do not make it on the ballot at all, and if they do, they receive little to no support.

Yet, when it comes to differentiating the "great" players who are elected to the Hall of Fame from the "very good" players who fall just short, there has been considerably less agreement among the members of the BBWAA. Since the Hall of Fame opened in 1936, there has been exactly one player who has received 100% support from the BBWAA—New York Yankees reliever Mariano Rivera, who was elected in 2019.

That means every other superstar in baseball history—from Babe Ruth to Ted Williams to Hank Aaron—had at least one BBWAA member who found some reason to vote no on their candidacy. Others did not even receive entry on their first year of eligibility. Joe DiMaggio, the New York Yankees center fielder and cultural icon who was married to Marilyn Monroe and immortalized in a Simon & Garfunkel song, was not elected until his third year on the ballot!

Sportswriter Joe Posnanski has described some baseball fans and BBWAA voters as proponents of what he calls "The Willie Mays Hall of Fame." Mays was a five-tool center fielder for the San Francisco Giants who many believe was the greatest player who ever lived. He is often evoked by people who argue against "lesser" stars' election to the Hall of Fame. The logic here is that Player X may have been a good player, but the Hall of Fame is supposed to be just for players like Willie Mays. However, as Posnanski noted, "Thing is, nobody's like Willie Mays. If he is the Hall of Fame standard, he's the only player in the Hall of Fame."[6]

A parallel can be drawn to assessing reviewers' publication recommendations. Some reviewers will only accept the "Willie Mays manuscripts"—those manuscripts that are truly exceptional and break new ground. Some reviewers will rarely, if ever, recommend conditionally accepting a manuscript on the first round of external review for the same reason that some BBWAA writers refuse to vote for any candidates appearing on the ballot for the first time—if DiMaggio did not get in on the first ballot, then no one should! Still other reviewers have a broader view of what constitutes an acceptable manuscript and argue that a well-theorized, methodologically sound study is worthy of publication, just as 75% of BBWAA writers believed that consistent, but not otherworldly, players like Al Simmons and Ralph Kiner deserved to be enshrined in Cooperstown.

In short, there is a line between accepted/elected and rejected/denied, but that line is not clear and looks different to every reviewer/BBWAA voter. To underscore this point, one more baseball example: Los Angeles Dodgers pitcher Don Drysdale was elected to the Hall of Fame in 1984 with 78% of the BBWAA vote on his 10th appearance on the ballot. He finished his career with a record of 209–166, a World Series championship, a Cy Young Award, multiple All-Star selections, and a record 58 scoreless inning streak.

Twenty-two years later, Orel Hershiser, who also pitched for the Dodgers, was on the Hall of Fame ballot for the first time. Hershiser had a record of 204–150, a World Series championship, a Cy Young Award, multiple All-Star selections, and actually broke Drysdale's scoreless innings record. Hershiser, however, only received 11% of the BBWAA vote in 2006 and completely fell off the ballot the following year.

Surely, there must be some qualitative difference between Drysdale and Hershiser to explain this vast discrepancy in vote totals, but many baseball fans have a hard time seeing it. Authors whose manuscripts are rejected likely feel the same way. It is certainly frustrating to receive an editorial decision with multiple interpretations from reviewers only to find that the editor has chosen to align with the reviewer who recommended rejection. Yet, the reviewer comments that the author sees only play a part in that decision-making. The next few sections discuss the various factors that determine how editors interpret reviewer comments and arrive at editorial decisions.

NAVIGATING REVIEWER COMMENTS AND PUBLICATION RECOMMENDATIONS

An important aspect of the peer review process that authors often do not realize is that reviewers are providing recommendations *to the editor*. Certainly, it is both collegial and instructive if reviewers craft their comments so that authors can benefit from them, but that is not their primary function. Instead, it is the editor who should bear the responsibility of communicating to authors through their decision letters.

As a general rule, it is a good practice for editors to avoid reading the reviewers' comments until after they have read the manuscript for themselves. However, it is often impossible, due to the way the journal management systems are constructed, to avoid seeing the reviewers' publication recommendations prior to reading the manuscript. So, editors often know if the reviewers are in agreement before delving into the manuscript.

Editors should approach the manuscript as an independent reviewer. It is not necessary to write detailed comments at this point; rather, this initial read should be for making general notes about the strengths and weaknesses of the manuscript. At the end of this read, editors can make an informal publication recommendation based on their initial dispositions toward the work. Of course, many of the manuscripts submitted to a journal extend beyond editors' specific areas of expertise, which is when the external reviewers become extremely valuable.

As noted in the previous chapter, the notion of "anonymous review" is a misnomer. Editors are aware of who the reviewers are and their level of expertise in a specific area of study. More importantly, after calling on the same reviewers over time, particularly members of their editorial boards, editors can get a sense of how "tough" they are with respect to their publication recommendations.

One *TRSE* editorial board member, for example, is a thorough reviewer who always writes extensive, constructive feedback. He almost always, however, recommends that manuscripts be rejected (he would be an example of the "Willie Mays Hall of Fame" mindset). Therefore, if he gives a manuscript a "reject, encourage resubmission" decision, it can be viewed as closer to an "accept with revisions" decision from someone else. Conversely, perhaps because many *TRSE* reviewers are former K-12 classroom teachers and education is a caring/loving profession, they often recommend "accept with revisions" but then proceed to list a litany of shortcomings that would require a major overhaul of the manuscript.

The point, then, is that reviewers' publication recommendations only reveal so much about their disposition toward a manuscript. Their narrative comments are more instructive. In most journal management systems, authors are given the opportunity to provide two sets of comments, one that is just for the editor and will not be shared with the author, and one that the author also sees.

Reviewers are often brutally honest in the comments that are exclusive to the editor (which is a good thing!) but may pull some of their punches in the comments to the author. For the purposes of collegiality, such an approach is valuable. However, it does result in less transparency given that the editor is sometimes unable to deftly incorporate reviewers' private comments into the decision letter that is sent to the author. As a result, authors may be more frustrated with a rejection when the reviews that they see do not appear overly negative.

When wading through reviewers' comments, editors can first see if they align with their initial read of the manuscript. If reviewers note the same strengths and weaknesses as the editor, particularly when a manuscript falls outside of the editor's area of scholarly expertise, they provide a baseline for comments to the author. The next step is to reread the reviewer comments, this time looking for areas of overlap with each other. As a general rule, if more than one reviewer mentions the same issue, it is worth addressing with the author.

Finally, editors should read the comments a third time with a critical eye toward finding places of disagreement and recognizing reviewer expertise. Not all reviewers are created equal. While all three reviewers will have expertise in some aspect of the manuscript, that expertise varies.

If, for example, the manuscript is about history education and uses historical consciousness as a theoretical framework, the expertise of the reviewer whose primary scholarly focus is historical consciousness should be valued when it comes to comments about the theoretical framework. Similarly, a different reviewer may not be well versed in the overall topic but was chosen to review the manuscript due to their methodological expertise; an editor will likely defer to their comments about methodology over the other reviewers.

Ultimately, interpreting reviewers' feedback is about creating a narrative of the manuscript by piecing together the best information at one's disposal. The editor has a great deal of latitude in crafting that narrative; they can choose to emphasize certain comments and disregard others. Once the narrative is established, the question then becomes whether it is one that can eventually lead to publication.

MAKING THE DECISION

As already noted, the decision-making process should go beyond just "averaging" the publication recommendations for two reasons:

- The publication recommendations mean different things to different reviewers.
- Reviewers can sometimes be wrong.

One manuscript submitted to *TRSE*, for example, had received two "accept with revisions" recommendations and one "reject" recommendation. The reviewer who recommended the manuscript be rejected had identified a significant methodological flaw that the other two reviewers (and I) had missed. Given that there was no way for the authors to remedy the methodological flaw at that point, I decided to reject the manuscript, and I explained my reasoning in the decision letter.

The harder cases are the ones in which the narrative is not as clear. A good rule of thumb for making manuscript decisions is to base the decision on two factors:

- Is there a reasonable pathway to publication for this manuscript?
- If so, how much work would it take to get it where it is deemed publishable?

While those may seem like fairly obvious questions, there is a little bit of editorial philosophy at play here.

Some editors are of the mindset that if there is even a speck of potential in a manuscript, then authors should be given a chance to revise and resubmit. While there is value in such a stance, there are ethical issues to consider. Unless an editor feels confident that the author can reasonably make the revisions needed to get the manuscript to the point it is publishable, it may be more "humane" to reject it outright rather than render a "reject, encourage resubmission" decision.

Getting rejected is never enjoyable, but having a revised manuscript rejected after a second round of external review really stings. More importantly, particularly for scholars on the tenure track, time becomes a factor. If the initial review process takes two months and then the author spends three months revising the manuscript followed by another two-month external review process, that is over a half a year wasted if the revision gets rejected (and many journals have much longer external review times). Had the manuscript been rejected outright, the author would instead be using that time to find a more suitable outlet for their work.

Determining whether a manuscript has a reasonable potential for publication is certainly subjective. However, it is wise to base that decision on what one can see in the manuscript and not what one hopes the author has at their disposal. In other words, if the revisions require a rethinking of the way the manuscript is framed or a complete rewriting of the analysis, then it may be reasonable for the author to make the necessary improvements. When revisions require additional data or when there are questions about the work's significance to the field, it is harder to make that determination.

Is this philosophy necessarily the correct one? Maybe not. All editors have failed to see the potential in some manuscripts that eventually became solid articles in other journals, and many articles now deemed classics in many disciplines started off being rejected by journals.[7] However, it is the most ethical approach to take.

That is not to say editors will never reject revised manuscripts; occasionally, authors are unable to satisfactorily respond to the concerns of the reviewers, and it leads to a rejection after the second round of external review. However, those rejections should be rare. The acceptance rate for *TRSE* manuscripts receiving a "reject, encourage resubmission" decision, for example, is over 80% as of this writing, so those difficult rejections do not happen often.

Another element of subjectivity comes in determining whether to conditionally accept a manuscript pending additional revisions or giving a "reject, encourage resubmission" decision and having the revised manuscript go out for another round of external review. As a general rule, it is wise to defer to the latter decision because once an author sees the word "accept," there is (or should be) an expectation that the manuscript will eventually be published. Therefore, one must be sure that the author can adequately respond to the requested revisions before rendering an "accept with revisions" decision.

An editor's own scholarly expertise can also play into this determination. Editors may be more likely to render a "reject, encourage resubmission" decision if a manuscript is not in their scholarly wheelhouse because they would not feel comfortable evaluating the revisions themselves. However, if the topic of a manuscript falls within an area in which they are knowledgeable, editors may choose to conditionally accept the manuscript knowing that they can work with the author "in house" to get the manuscript to the point where it is deemed publishable.

Again, as a general rule, it is safer and more prudent to require another round of external review—at least on the initial decision. Where the choice between "accept with revisions" and "reject, encourage resubmission" becomes particularly important is when one is evaluating a revised manuscript that has already gone through two cycles of external review.

It is not ethical to make an author go through more than one revise and resubmit cycle without a guarantee of acceptance, so if the manuscript has improved to the point where one can see a clear path to publication, then an "accept with revisions" decision is appropriate. However, if the author has not adequately responded to the reviewers' concerns from the first round of external review, it may be better to reject the manuscript outright at that point.

On rare occasions, I have rendered a "reject, encourage resubmission" decision on the second round of external review. In those cases, the manuscripts were improved from the first iteration, but there were still areas where significant revisions were needed. To be transparent to the authors (and to encourage them to engage in another round of revision), I would include the following in my decision letter:

> While the revised manuscript will go out for another round of external review and acceptance is not guaranteed, I am always cognizant of not wanting to string authors along with multiple rounds of revision without a conditional acceptance. Therefore, I make you this promise: If you decide to revise and resubmit back to *TRSE*, the next decision will either be "accept with revisions" or "reject."

CONVEYING DECISIONS TO AUTHORS

All of the thought and effort that goes into making an editorial decision means little if it is not communicated to the author effectively. Oftentimes, editors simply render an editorial decision and provide authors with the reviewers' comments without any detailed synthesis or direction forward. In addition to compounding authors' frustration, this lack of specificity is particularly detrimental when rendering an "accept with revisions" or "reject, encourage resubmission" decision as it increases the likelihood that authors will fail to submit a revised manuscript that addresses all of the editor's concerns.

A detailed editorial decision letter, then, is essential to both author satisfaction and ensuring quality publications. I have provided two examples of a typical editorial decision letter from my tenure at *TRSE* in Appendices B and C. They are both letters for "reject, encourage resubmission" decisions; in both cases, the author then submitted a revision, and the revised manuscript was conditionally accepted for publication after the subsequent round of external review and published soon thereafter.[8] This general format can be used for all "reject"; "reject, encourage resubmission"; and "accept with revisions" decisions.

It is important to quickly convey to authors what they are most interested in—the reviewers' recommendations and the overall editorial outcome. Providing the reviewers' publication recommendations provides a level of transparency for authors (although on those occasions when the editorial decision goes against that of the majority of reviewers, then it may make the editor the target of authors' ire!). When there is a great deal of consistency within the reviewers' narrative comments, it is worth alerting authors to that consistency despite the reviewers offering differing publication recommendations.

When it comes to issuing an editorial decision, it is important to let authors know that the editor has read the manuscript and that their decision is made in consultation with, but not solely reliant on, the reviewers' comments and publication recommendations. It is easy for an editor to hide behind the recommendations of the reviewers, but doing so obfuscates the decision-making power that an editor has.[9] Ultimately, the publication decision rests with the editor, so it is important that the editor clearly owns that decision.

Even when rendering a "reject" decision, it is good form to note a couple of interesting aspects of the manuscript before letting the author know that "the current limitations in the manuscript are beyond what is typical for a 'reject, encourage resubmission' decision," and for that reason the "editorial decision is to reject the manuscript." For "reject, encourage resubmission" decisions, it is important to be as specific as possible in projecting the level of confidence that the manuscript will ultimately be accepted for publication.

As one can see in the letters found in Appendices B and C, I noted that I saw a pathway forward to publication in *TRSE*, but for it to get there, the author would need to engage in major revisions, and I listed specific sections of the manuscript that needed to be revised. When an editor is not as confident in the prospects for publication, they may instead say something like

The topic of the manuscript is one that is both of interest to *TRSE* readers and underrepresented within social studies research (and the pages of *TRSE*). That said, I think the manuscript needs a lot of work, and I have some concerns about the amount of data you collected (or lack thereof), which always makes me nervous when I think about rendering a "reject, encourage resubmission" decision. Typically, I only render that decision if I feel confident that the manuscript could get to the point it is deemed publishable in *TRSE*, and I can't say that about this manuscript. That said, given the importance of the topic, I am willing to give you a shot at revising the manuscript, if you so choose.

This type of blunt assessment is not intended to dissuade authors from resubmitting; on the contrary, editors should only render a "reject, encourage resubmission" decision because they see something of interest in the work. Yet, providing a realistic assessment of the likelihood of publication is the most ethical practice. Authors can then make an informed decision about how to proceed with their work.

For those manuscripts that are hovering in that space between "accept with revisions" and "reject, encourage resubmission" but cannot yet be conditionally accepted, it is useful to provide some emphasis that lets authors know that they really should resubmit. Typically, I use bold italics font and write something like, "***I strongly encourage you to revise and resubmit the manuscript back to TRSE*** if you believe you can adequately address the concerns made by the reviewers and the issues I raise in this letter." At times, I have even written something along the lines of "If we had a decision category of 'accept with major revisions,' I would probably assign it here; however, given my lack of expertise in the subject, I want to send it out for another round of external review."

It is also important to convey exactly what these editorial decisions mean. Most seasoned authors have received a message from a journal editor that says something like: "The reviewer(s) have recommended publication, but also suggest some major revisions to your manuscript. Therefore, I invite you to respond to the reviewer(s)' comments and revise your manuscript." It is not clear what that statement means. Is the manuscript conditionally accepted? Will the revised manuscript be sent back out for another round of external review? Such vague language does not provide authors with any useful information.

Authors need to know that "reject, encourage resubmission" decisions (or "revise/resubmit") involve further rounds of external review without any guarantee of acceptance. Yet, an "accept with revisions" decision means that the manuscript will eventually be published, but it may take multiple rounds of revision to get it there. Authors usually understand what a "reject" decision means, but occasionally authors whose manuscripts have been rejected try to resubmit. One way to hammer the point home is to provide the names of alternative journals to which they can send their manuscripts.

PROVIDING A CLEAR NARRATIVE TO AUTHORS

After clarifying the publication decision, the main function of the editorial decision letter is to provide authors with a road map for how to improve the manuscript. As in Appendices B and C, occasionally manuscripts have an overarching issue that affects multiple sections of the piece. In those cases, it makes sense to address the overarching issue first and then move on to a detailed discussion of each individual section of the manuscript.

The key here is to be as specific as possible without overwhelming the author.[10] As the sample letters in Appendices B and C show, it helps to highlight specific comments made by reviewers that are particularly salient. Also, when asking authors to improve their literature review or theoretical framework, it is helpful to provide names of relevant scholars or even specific citations that would be useful to their argument. It is also the editor's job to weigh in when reviewers disagree about an aspect of the manuscript.

The most difficult requests to make of an author are ones that ask them to reframe aspects of their argument or present their work in fundamentally different ways. Particularly if the manuscript has been reviewed fairly positively, authors may bristle at being asked to make substantive changes. However, as Nicholas Burbules, former editor of the journal *Educational Theory*, noted, journal editors have to weigh the preferences of authors with "a respect for the audience(s) of a journal and what will communicate to them; what they will have the patience to struggle through, or not, in order to extract meaning from an article."[11]

These types of asks often come when authors are employing a methodology not common to the field or writing in a genre that defies typical practices. For example, a relatively small, but growing, cadre of scholars in social studies education has embraced postqualitative research, and consequently, *TRSE* has begun receiving postqualitative studies in recent years.[12] Oftentimes, these manuscripts are thought-provoking and address important issues within the field, and as such, they have been accepted.[13]

Yet, just because a journal is open to a range of methodologies and writing styles does not mean that manuscripts should be published without the "typical" reader in mind. If only a small subset of readers will be familiar with a certain methodology or genre of scholarship, then it means that the overall impact of the article will suffer because it will only speak to those who already agree with the particular stance presented in the article.

While an editor should never demand a complete change of methodology or style, it is reasonable to ask authors to compromise a little in order to ensure greater accessibility for the general reader. As Burbules argued, "the audience's interests, and the interests of the journal generally in being regarded as readable and accessible, trump the preferences of the author to simply say what he or she wants to say in whatever way he or she wants to say it."[14]

As Appendices B and C show, the bulk of an editorial decision letter should focus on broad issues, as opposed to minute details such as word choice or grammatical mistakes. However, for "reject, encourage resubmission" or "accept with revisions" decisions, it is useful to end a decision letter with a list of minor issues that were particularly glaring or repeated throughout the manuscript. These types of minor issues include things like improper citation practices, failure to follow appropriate style guidelines, or procedural issues related to tables and figures.

Until a manuscript is conditionally accepted, it is not worth spending time worrying about the accuracy of references or things like copyright permissions for figures. However, at the end of "accept with revisions" decisions, including a "preparing the manuscript for publication" checklist for authors to complete before submitting the final version of the manuscript can make the production part of the publication process much smoother. An example of this type of checklist can be found in Appendix D.

OTHER CONSIDERATIONS

There are a few other considerations that editors must make during the decision-making process. One is whether to censor any aspects of the reviewers' comments before sending them to the author. In general, it is best practice to convey reviewers' comments as they were written; success in academia is about developing thick skin and being receptive to critical feedback. Yet, as noted in the previous chapter, manuscripts about certain topics (e.g., race) may elicit more problematic comments than others, and even with manuscripts on noncontroversial topics, one may end up with a rude reviewer.

Being judicious in one's selection of reviewers can help alleviate potential issues, but occasionally comments that cross the line from constructive to mean-spirited do get made. In my experience with *TRSE*, such comments are rare, and I have had to censor a reviewer's feedback only a handful of times.

The instances that immediately come to mind are ones in which a reviewer states, in the public comments to the author, that they believe the author is a graduate student when, in fact, the author is a second- or third-year assistant professor. This type of "feedback" is not constructive and is not directly related to improving the manuscript. Given the potential for such comments to be needlessly demoralizing, editors may choose to remove them before sending the feedback to the authors.

Another consideration when rendering an "accept with revisions" or a "reject, encourage resubmission" decision is to give authors some leeway on page limits or word counts. Anyone who has ever been asked to revise a manuscript has felt the frustration of being told by editors and reviewers to add information to a manuscript that is already pushing the word/page limit while simultaneously being told to make sure that the revised manuscript adheres to the journal's submission requirements.

Rules are made to be bent, and if possible, editors can choose to give authors room to expand on their argument in light of reviewer feedback. However, if contractual page requirements prevent this type of leeway, then it is incumbent on the editor to tell authors which revisions to prioritize or give suggestions on where they can cut words in the revised manuscript.

IMPLICATIONS FOR AUTHORS

Few authors have any knowledge of the thought processes that editors go through when making a decision on a manuscript. After reading this chapter, what should authors glean from it? Here are some takeaways, in order of importance:

Always Take the Revise/Resubmit Option If Given to You

Editors often have to console novice scholars who have received a "reject, encourage resubmission" decision and have focused only on the "reject" part of the decision. It is important to remember that a conditional acceptance after the first round of external review is exceedingly rare (especially for top-tier journals), and if one is given an opportunity to resubmit, then authors should view that as *good news*. Even when the revisions being asked for are daunting, it is almost always in one's best interest to attempt a revision instead of starting over with a new journal.

At a basic level, it is a numbers game. The acceptance rate for a revised manuscript is much higher than for initial submissions. Also, an editor will almost always send a revised manuscript back to at least one (if not all) of the original reviewers; therefore, authors are starting with reviewers who are familiar with the manuscript and can see its improvement over time. Finally, that the editor allowed an opportunity for revision indicates that they see value in the research and are hopeful that the manuscript will ultimately be published. Given that they make the final decision, the fact that the editor has a positive disposition about the revised manuscript from the outset increases the likelihood of success.

Follow the Editor's Lead—And Learn to Read Between the Lines

When an author receives multiple comprehensive reviews, along with a detailed editorial decision letter, trying to wade through all of that feedback can seem overwhelming. It is important, then, when given the opportunity to revise a manuscript, to prioritize the revisions. Always start with the editor's synthesis and specific recommendations. Remember, they know who the reviewers are and whose recommendations should be prioritized. In other words, if an editor does not explicitly note a suggestion made by a specific reviewer, then it may be something that the author can argue is not essential. On the other hand, if the editor explicitly notes something to fix, then it is in the author's best interest to do so.

This prioritization is also important when composing the response letter that will accompany a revised manuscript. This letter can take many forms—a narrative, a chart, a table—but it should pick apart individual recommendations made by both the editor and each reviewer and explain how the author did or did not address them. Authors should know that they *do not* have to agree with every suggestion made by the editor or reviewers. However, if they disagree with a specific suggestion, they should explain why and just not ignore it.

One additional note about this response letter: It should be anonymized. This letter will likely accompany the revised manuscript when sent to the reviewers, so it should not have any identifying information in it, nor should it be submitted on university letterhead. Submitting a deanonymized response letter is a red flag to an editor that an author is a novice at scholarly publishing. Also, if the editor does not catch the lack of anonymization and sends the manuscript to the original reviewers, who then alert the editor to the breech in anonymous review, the revision will be sent to a completely new slate of reviewers, which hurts the chances of acceptance.

Finally, do not just accept the editor's comments at face value; *how* they write the decision letter often says as much as the editorial decision itself. This ability to read between the lines is particularly important for "reject, encourage resubmission" decisions. Does the editor seem enthusiastic about the possibility of publishing the manuscript, or are they just giving you a shot because there *might* be some potential there? Are they minimizing a reviewer's suggestion without coming right out and saying it (because they may not want to offend the reviewer)? Picking up on these subtle hints can help with both the revision process and tempering expectations of success.

Don't Get Hung Up on Reviewers' Publication Recommendations—Focus on Their Comments

Just as editors should take reviewers' publication recommendations with a grain of salt, authors should also recognize the inherent subjectivity behind these recommendations. Authors have no idea whether an individual reviewer has a "Wille Mays Hall of Fame" disposition and will never conditionally accept something on the first round of review or has a "Big Hall" philosophy. Therefore, it is a pointless endeavor to try to make determinations about the quality of one's manuscript based on these publication recommendations, nor should authors prioritize the suggestions of reviewers who recommended "reject" or "reject, encourage resubmission" over those who recommended "accept with revisions."

Authors should instead focus on the reviewers' comments. If the reviewers' suggestions align, despite differing publication recommendations, then every effort should be made to remedy those concerns. This advice holds even if the manuscript is rejected. Many academic disciplines are relatively small, and subfields within disciplines can often be exclusive. Therefore, it is not unusual for the same reviewer to be selected to review the same manuscript by different journal editors. If that reviewer does not see where the author has attended to the suggestions made at the earlier journal, the chances of success with the new submission are diminished.

Don't Take Rejection as Evidence That a Manuscript is Fundamentally Flawed

Economist Richard Freeman noted that

> everyone has a "good" paper rejected at one time because of a vicious unfair stupid referee, and everyone has a "bad" paper rejected at one time because it deserves to be buried. Neither are quite as devastating as a teenager being rejected in some passionate one-sided romance, but you still can't forget them.[15]

Indeed, rejections sting, and it is not uncommon to want to completely give up on a manuscript after it has been rejected. Doing so, however, is short sighted. Editorial decisions are imperfect predictions, and many editors adopt the philosophy of only giving an opportunity to resubmit if the manuscript has a clear pathway to publication. Therefore, it is entirely possible that a rejected manuscript can be salvaged and published elsewhere.

Freeman also acknowledged that there is some relief that one gets from a rejection: "the certain knowledge that the editor and referees are blind baseball umpires, members of The Three Stooges, or incompetents in even more drastic ways."[16] Freeman obviously made that comment tongue-in-cheek; while it soothing to believe that everyone who recommended that the manuscript be rejected is a moron, the reality is that they probably noticed some fundamental flaws in the work that need to be remedied. A good rule of thumb is to put negative reviews in a drawer for a few days and then reread them with fresh eyes; often they appear more reasonable once the initial emotions have waned.

Even if one is convinced the editor and reviewers got it completely wrong, it is unwise to just take the rejected manuscript and submit it to another journal without engaging in some revisions based on the feedback given from the original journal for the reasons given above. Yet, authors have more leeway here to ignore comments perceived as "incorrect" than they do when revising and resubmitting. In choosing where to send the manuscript next, if the editor from the first journal offered suggestions, they are worth considering. Editors tend to know the field and what types of manuscripts are appropriate for different journals.

As a rule of thumb, once a manuscript is rejected from a journal, it makes little sense to submit it to a more prestigious journal. It is fine, however, to take a chance with a journal that is on equal footing with the one that rendered the reject decision. If, however, the manuscript is rejected from the second journal, it is likely time to submit it to a less prestigious journal. In general, a manuscript should not be considered a "failure" until it has been rejected by three journals. Even then, do not give up hope! It is still possible to find a home for the piece, although significant reworking is likely required.

A FINAL NOTE

Both editors and authors should know that editors do not always get it right. To err is human, and I am sure that over the years, I have misread manuscripts and made decisions that were too harsh or too lenient. As this chapter has shown, the process of coming to an editorial decision on a manuscript is difficult, influenced by a variety of factors, and inherently subjective. Yet, when implemented correctly, an editorial decision represents a good-faith, thoughtful effort to do what is best for both the journal and the author.

NOTES

1. To the best of my recollection, all three reviewers recommending "accept, pending revision" after the first round of external review has occurred exactly one time during my time editing *TRSE*.

2. See, for example, Alison M. Konrad, "Knowledge Creation and the Journal Editor's Role," in *Opening the Black Box of Editorship,* ed. Yehuda Baruch, Alison M. Konrad, Herman Aguinis, and William H. Starbuck (New York: Palgrave MacMillan, 2008), 3–15; Wollf-Michael Roth, "Editorial: On Editing and Being an Editor," *Cultural Studies of Science Education* 1 (2006): 209–17, https://doi.org/10.1007/s11422 -006-9024-y.

3. Konrad, "Knowledge Creation," 9.

4. Clarivate, "Web of Science Journal Evaluation Process and Selection Criteria," accessed July 6, 2022, https://clarivate.com/products/scientific-and-academic -research/research-discovery-and-workflow-solutions/web-of-science/core-collection /editorial-selection-process/editorial-selection-process/.

5. "BBWAA Election Rules," National Baseball Hall of Fame, accessed June 23, 2022, https://baseballhall.org/hall-of-famers/rules/bbwaa-rules-for-election.

6. Joe Posnanski, *The Baseball 100* (New York: Avid Reader Press, 2021), 826.

7. See, for example, Joshua S. Gans and George B. Shepherd, "How Are the Mighty Fallen: Rejected Classic Articles by Leading Economists," *The Journal of Economic Perspectives* 8, no. 1 (1994): 165–79.

8. Emma S. Thacker and Aaron T. Bodle, "Seizing the Moment: A Critical Place-Based Partnership for Antiracist Elementary Social Studies Teacher Education," *Theory & Research in Social Education* 50, no. 2 (2022), 402–30; Jon M. Wargo, "'Sound' Civics, Heard Histories: A Critical Case of Young Children Mobilizing Digital Media to Write (Right) Injustice," *Theory & Research in Social Education* 49, no. 3 (2021), 360–89, https://doi.org/10.1080/00933104.2021.1874582.

9. Wollf-Michael Roth, "Editorial Power/Authorial Suffering," *Research in Science Education* 32 (2002): 229–31, https://doi.org/10.1023/A:1016030212572.

10. Sara L. Rynes, "Communicating with Authors," in *Opening the Black Box of Editorship,* ed. Yehuda Baruch, Alison M. Konrad, Herman Aguinis, and William H. Starbuck (New York: Palgrave MacMillan, 2008), 56–67.

11. Nicholas C. Burbules, "Philosophical Reflections on Editing," *Educational Theory* 64, no. 4 (2014): 325, https://doi.org/10.1111/edth.12069.

12. For those unfamiliar with postqualitative research, see Alecia Y. Jackson and Lisa A. Mazzei, *Thinking With Theory in Qualitative Research: Viewing Data Across Multiple Perspectives* (New York: Routledge, 2012).

13. Examples of *TRSE* articles that use postqualitative approaches include Gerardo Joel Aponte-Safe, Ana Carolina Díaz Beltrán, and Rebecca C. Christ, "Aspiring Nepantleras: Conceptualizing Social Studies Education from the Rupture/La Herida Abierta," *Theory & Research in Social Education* 50, no. 1 (2022): 74–100, https:// doi.org/10/1080/00933104.2021.2009948 and Sarah B. Shear and Daniel G. Krutka, "Confronting Settler Colonialism: Theoretical and Methodological Questions About Social Studies Research," *Theory & Research in Social Education* 47, no. 1 (2019): 29–51, https://doi.org/10.1080/00933104.2018.1541428.

14. Burbules, "Philosophical Reflections," 326.

15. Gans and Shepherd, "How Are the Mighty," 178.

16. Gans and Shepherd, "How Are the Mighty," 177.

Chapter 5

Marketing Articles and Making an Impact

For authors, receiving news of a manuscript's acceptance marks the end of a long, often frustrating process. They usually celebrate, add the new publication to their vita, and move on to the next project. For editors, however, a manuscript acceptance starts a new phase of the publication journey that arguably involves more work than the external review process. This chapter describes what happens post–manuscript acceptance, from copyediting to marketing articles on social media.

COPYEDITING

Now that most journals are housed within global publishing companies, a common misnomer about journal editing is that once a manuscript is accepted, the publisher does all of the work. Without question, publishers take care of a lot of headaches (e.g., formatting tables/figures, typesetting articles) that editors used to do themselves. Editors, however, still have a prominent role in the production process.

Once a manuscript is officially accepted, it does not automatically go to the publisher. Editors have the opportunity to do a first round of copyediting on their own. Some editors eschew this responsibility, but doing so will likely lead to a greater number of errors that make it through to the published article. The publisher's copyediting process is highly automated, and it does not make changes in terms of readability or coherence. Therefore, an initial read-through by the editor is recommended to catch errors and smooth out authors' writing.

As noted in the previous chapter, it is good practice to have authors deanonymize the manuscript as they complete their last round of revisions. Leaving the deanonymizing to the publisher often results in one or more "Author,

XXXX" citations remaining within the body of the published manuscript. Once the manuscript is deanonymized, and in what the author believes to be the manuscript's final form, editors can begin to engage in a line-by-line copyediting of the manuscript. During this process, editors should look for the following:

- Grammatical mistakes/typos
- Failure to deanonymize the manuscript
- Citation style mistakes
- Instances of poor writing
- References that are incomplete/incorrect

Assuming the journal is housed within a publishing agency, it is usually not necessary to cross-check references with citations. The publisher's automated process will find those errors.

As already noted, many excellent scholars are not great writers. Moreover, many international researchers writing outside of their native language may submit manuscripts that constitute quality research, but the writing leaves much to be desired. As such, most authors expect—and appreciate—a certain amount of wordsmithing by editors prior to publication. The question becomes how much rewriting by editors is appropriate?

The general rule of thumb to follow is that if an edit improves readability but does not change the author's meaning or intent, it is fine to make the change. Of course, one way to ensure that authors are fine with editorial changes is to ask permission via email or send them a copy of the edited manuscript with track changes. The downside of this approach is that it creates more work for both the editor and author, and it extends the time to publication. Therefore, if edits are minor and simply made for aesthetic purposes, it is often fine to implement them and let authors make changes at the page proof stage.

When in doubt, *ask permission from authors* before making any substantive changes. An accepted manuscript may become copyrighted to the journal, but it is still the author's intellectual work. Substantively editing a manuscript to the point that it changes an author's meaning or intent is unethical. Even certain stylistic decisions, such as capitalizing Black and/or White, sometimes are made purposefully by authors. It is fine to let authors know if they have violated journal or citation style policies and that they need to make the necessary changes, but an editor should never make such changes on their own.[1]

Once editors have completed their copyedit, it is time to send the manuscript to the publisher for yet another round of copyediting. Again, this part of the process is highly automated and results in page proofs that are typically sent to both the editor and author for review. The publisher will note any errors they have found, usually through queries that the author is asked to resolve. The more a manuscript is copyedited prior to sending to the publisher, usually the fewer number of queries that are generated.

By this point, between multiple rounds of revision and copyediting the accepted manuscript, editors have read several versions of the accepted manuscript. It is tempting, then, to just skim the page proofs or rely on the author to catch any mistakes that may exist. However, one would be shocked at how often the page proofs contain errors ranging from spacing issues to obvious typos. The page proofs are the last opportunity to make the article perfect, so it is wise to take them seriously. The reputation of the journal is at stake; potential authors who see multiple errors in articles will be less likely to submit their work there.

IMPACT/CITATION METRICS

Even after an article is published, there is still more work to be done. Journals (and, increasingly, scholars) are judged on how often their articles are read and cited. Unfortunately, there is no universally agreed upon metric to determine the "health" of a journal. Here are the most common metrics used in the world of academic journal publishing, all of which have strengths and limitations.

Article Downloads

Perhaps the most straightforward metric is the number of article downloads that a journal has in any given year. Obviously, more downloads mean that a greater number of people are interacting with journal content. Perhaps the greatest strength of using downloads as an analytical tool is that it can provide editors and publishers a sense of what topics within the journal are getting the most traction. That information can be used to inform future editorial efforts, such as the formation of special issues or encouraging scholars who research that topic to submit their work to the journal.

Another strength of downloads is that they provide publishers with information about where they were accessed, which can allow publishers and editors to better determine the global reach of the journal. Such information is useful for journals that are international in scope. If an editor sees that there is great interest in the journal in a certain country or region, they can seek out scholars from that area to perhaps serve on the editorial board, which will hopefully lead to a greater number of submissions.

One limitation of downloads is that they only account for readers who interact with the journal online. Although more people are reading electronic versions of journal articles than ever before, many still prefer to read hard copies, and there is no way to monitor that type of article consumption. Also, just because an article is downloaded does not mean it is read, and the number of downloads does not provide any indication of *who* is reading it. Are students downloading an article because it is required reading for one of their classes? Or is the article being read by scholars who are likely to cite it in their own work? More information is needed to discern whether downloads mean that the research published in a journal will advance the field.

Impact Factor

Most journal metrics involve tracking article citations. By far, the most used—and most controversial—of those metrics is the impact factor.[2] Calculating a journal's impact factor is straightforward; it is the number of approved citations received in one year of content published in the previous two years divided by the total number of articles published within the previous two years. For example, a journal's 2022 impact factor would be calculated by taking the number of approved citations in 2022 of articles published in 2020 and 2021 divided by the total number of articles published in 2020 and 2021.

So, if in 2022, a journal had 350 citations of articles published in 2020 and 250 citations of articles published in 2021, that would be 600 total articles that would count toward the journal's impact factor. Any citations of journal content prior to 2020 would not count. Then, if the journal published 20 articles in both 2020 and 2021, those 40 articles would serve as the denominator in the equation. Dividing 600 by 40 results in an impact factor of 15.

While many journals may report an impact factor, only journals admitted into Clarivate's Science Citation Index Expanded (SCIE), Social Science Citation Index (SSCI), or Arts and Humanities Citation Index (AHCI) receive an official impact factor. Admission into these indexes is highly competitive and based on a number of factors relating to the quality of a journal. Although the criteria are always changing, as of this writing, inclusion in the SCIE, SSCI, or AHCI is influenced by the following factors[3]:

- The journal must have a registered International Standard Serial Number
- The journal must have a distinct title aligned with the journal's stated scope
- The journal must have a legitimate publisher
- The journal must have a website that provides options for full-text content (and Clarivate must be given access to that content)
- The journal must have a clear commitment to peer review and/or editorial oversight of all published content

- The journal's primary editorial and production roles must have clear contact details
- The journal must publish original scholarly material that is appropriate to graduate, postdoctoral, and/or professional research audiences
- All article titles and abstracts must be in English (or have an English translation)
- Bibliographic information must be published in Roman script
- All published text must be clear and comprehensible to a global audience
- The journal must have a defined publication schedule, and it must conform to that schedule
- The volume of scholarly articles published annually should demonstrate that the journal is attracting sufficient interest from its respective field
- The journal's website must be accurate and ensure easy access to published content, as well as information related to peer review, author instructions, etc.
- The journal must be transparent about its ethical requirements for authors and published work, and all published content should demonstrate adherence to these policies
- The journal's editorial board members are identifiable, with names and institutional affiliations (including country/region) clearly noted
- Authors of all scholarly work published in the journal must be accurately identified, along with their institutional information
- The editorial team and editorial board affiliations, geographic diversity, and publication records must be consistent with the stated scope of the journal
- Content published in the journal must reflect adequate and effective peer review and/or editorial oversight
- Content published in the journal must be relevant to the scope of the journal
- If research published in the journal is funded by grants, acknowledgment of the funding source is recommended
- The journal's editorial policies are consistent with best practices for research integrity
- Authors publishing in the journal must have affiliations, geographic diversity, and publication records that validate their participation in the field associated with the journal
- Articles published in the journal must appropriately acknowledge the extant literature on the topic of focus
- Journals must be well cited, as well as show a stable number of citations over time
- Most authors published in the journal should have a discernible publication history in the Web of Science[4]

- The journal's editorial board members should have a discernible publication history in the Web of Science
- The journal's content should be of interest, importance, and value to its respective field

As one can see, some of these requirements are procedural and fairly easy to achieve; others are more subjective and reliant on the quality of content the journal publishes. Journals that feel as though they meet all of these criteria can apply to Clarivate for inclusion. Accepted journals are first placed in Clarivate's Emerging Sources Citation Index (ESCI) where they are monitored for an undefined amount of time.

Journals in the ESCI do not receive an official impact factor; however, if the journal's citation metrics during their time in the ESCI show that they are in the top half of the journals in their relevant categories, they are then promoted to either the SCIE, SSCI, or AHCI where they will receive an official impact factor.[5] It is important to note, though, that inclusion in the SCIE, SSCI, or AHCI is not necessarily permanent. Journals in these indexes are constantly monitored, and if the quality of their publications or number of citations slip significantly, they can be demoted back to the ESCI.

Given this rigorous and uncertain vetting process, it may be tempting to ask why editors should even bother applying for inclusion. The answer is that, for better or worse, the impact factor has become the gold standard for evaluating academic publishing, and journals that do not have an official impact factor are often at a disadvantage when it comes to receiving high-quality manuscripts. Many colleges and universities are increasingly using journal impact factors as part of promotion and tenure decisions, which means that scholars at those institutions are more likely to seek out journals with official impact factors, at least while they are on the tenure track.

Also, inclusion in the SCIE, SSCI, or AHCI brings much greater visibility for a journal. These indexes are valued around the world, so when a journal is accepted for inclusion, its number of submissions is almost certainly to increase. Moreover, the more global focus can also lead to more downloads and a greater diversity of thought within the pages of the journal.

The impact factor, however, also has significant limitations when used to assess the quality of a journal. The two-year calculation window penalizes journals in smaller fields and fields that do not prioritize rapid publication of articles. Many of the journals in the fields of medicine or science, for example, review manuscripts and publish them online within weeks, which, as during the COVID-19 pandemic, is useful in aiding policymakers' decisions about public health. A recently published article in the journal *Nature*, for example, was submitted on December 7, 2021, accepted on December 23,

2021, and published online that same day.[6] Perhaps not surprisingly, *Nature*'s impact factor, as of this writing, is 49.96.

Compare that impact factor with journals in the humanities, which often publish quarterly issues. Even with the advent of online preprints, the publication time does not come close to that of the hard sciences. Consider, for example, the journal *Review of Educational Research*, which, as of this writing, has the highest impact factor of all journals within the field of education and educational research. Its impact factor is "only" 12.56.

A journal's impact factor can also be skewed due to an unusually highly cited article falling within that two-year calculation window. That article will cause the impact factor to temporarily spike, but after the calculation window passes, the impact factor will decrease accordingly. Smaller journals are more prone to these types of drastic fluctuations than larger journals due to having a smaller number of articles in the denominator of the calculation. As a result, many critics have argued that the impact factor is not an accurate measure of a journal's impact on a field.

A final limitation of the impact factor is that it does not "count" all citations in its calculations. Only citations in journals indexed in the ESCI, SCIE, SSCI, and AHCI count towards journal impact factors, which penalizes journals in fields that only have one indexed journal. For example, the journal that cites the most *TRSE* articles is the *Journal of Social Studies Research* (*JSSR*). However, as of this writing, *JSSR* has not been admitted into any Clarivate indexes; therefore, its citations of *TRSE* articles do not improve *TRSE*'s impact factor.

Five-Year Impact Factor

The five-year impact factor is calculated the same way as the regular impact factor only it uses a five-year instead of a two-year window. The five-year window provides a fairer calculation for those fields of study, such as the humanities, that take longer to publish. By using a five-year window, more citations can be accumulated over time. However, the five-year impact factor has the same limitations as the regular impact factor.

CiteScore

A journal's CiteScore is another calculation of citations, but it uses Scopus, which is a competitor to Clarivate that is owned by the publishing company Elsevier. The CiteScore calculation works in much the same way as the impact factor, but instead of focusing only on citations in academic journals, it also includes citations in books, conference papers, and other types of academic work.[7] It also uses a four-year calculation window, as opposed to the two-year window for the impact factor.

By using more sources in its calculation, the CiteScore provides a more comprehensive analysis of a journal's impact. This expanded scope is particularly valuable in fields that value publishing books and conference proceedings. Also, even when focusing just on journal articles, the Scopus database is not as exclusive as Clarivate's. Therefore, the number of citations a journal has accrued from other journals will be more accurate.

Of course, CiteScore is subjected to many of the same limitations as the impact factor given the similarities in calculation formulas. Just like with the impact factor, a journal's CiteScore can be skewed by an unusually popular article, and although four years is more generous than two, journals in more methodical fields will have lower scores than those that prioritize rapid publication.

SCImago Journal Rank

The SCImago Journal Rank (SJR) is a measure of journal impact that uses the Scopus database. It is run by the SCImago research group, which is housed in Spain. What makes the SJR different is that it does not count all citations equally; rather, it weighs the prestige of the citing journal. In other words, a citation from a journal ranked highly in the SJR is "worth" more than a citation that has a lesser rank. It uses a three-year calculation window.

On one hand, the SJR provides a little more subjectivity than what is found in either the impact factor or CiteScore. However, the weights given to journals is calculated through an algorithm that is largely based on citations. Using a complicated mathematical formula, the SJR monitors how journals "transfer" prestige to other journals through citations.[8]

H-Index

Finally, the h-index is a measure created by physicist Jorge Hirsch that can be used to quantify the impact of both journals and individual scholars. The h-index is calculated by the number of papers (represented by h) that have been cited at least h times. For example, if a journal has published 30 articles that have each been cited at least 30 times, then their h-index is 30. If the journal's 31st most cited article has only been cited 29 times, then the h-index remains 30. Once that 31st most cited article reaches 31 citations, then the h-index would become 31.

One benefit of the h-index, as opposed to both the impact factor and CiteScore, is that it does not allow for skewing based on a handful of highly cited articles. As a result, it gives a better approximation of how likely any given article might expect to be cited in a particular journal. One limitation, however, of the h-index is that there is no set requirement on which databases should be used to determine it. Calculating a journal's h-index using the Clarivate indexes will almost certainly lead to a lower h-index than if one uses Scopus.

WHAT TRULY CONSTITUTES IMPACT?

Wading through these various metrics is enough to give any editor a headache. Moreover, much of a journal's "impact" is out of an editor's control. Editors have some influence over the content a journal publishes, but they cannot dictate how often articles in their journals are read or cited. Citations rely on the scholarly awareness—and publication skill—of others, so editors should not obsess over these metrics. Certainly, these numbers shed insight about the success/health of a journal, but they often do not reveal the entire picture.

It is also important to remember that not all forms of impact can be measured by a mathematical equation. If a mainstream news outlet discovers a journal article and incorporates its findings as part of a story, then that article is likely making a far greater impact than if academics are simply citing it as part of their scholarly publications. Similarly, if a journal caters to a field, such as teaching or nursing, that seeks to improve clinical practice, getting articles in the hands of policymakers can lead to the types of practical impact that cannot be found in an impact factor or CiteScore.

The better way to think about impact, then, is to worry less about what people do with the articles and instead focus on how to make journal content more accessible to the masses. If people do not engage with journal content, then it certainly will not be influential, no matter how one is defining "impact." Today, academic journals face unprecedented competition for readers' attention. New journals seemingly emerge daily, and they are all competing for the same readers, who have a limited amount of time and resources to consume new information.

Therefore, if editors want their journals to have an impact, then it is essential that their journals stand out from the crowd. Some journals will be able to get their content in front of readers without much effort due to the historical prestige they have developed over time. Other journals will need to work harder or be more creative. The next section offers ways in which editors can promote their journals and make their content more likely to be found and read.

JOURNAL MARKETING

Marketing is an unheralded aspect of journal editing. It often takes place behind the scenes, and unlike the editorial decision-making process, which tends to occur in waves, marketing requires a consistent effort. A steady flow of marketing is much more effective than short spurts of intense coverage of journal content. Journals published by commercial publishing houses can engage their publisher's help with marketing, but given the volume of journals published by these companies, much of the work will fall to the editor. Here are some strategies that editors can employ to market journal content.

Social Media

We live in an era defined by social media. Recent surveys have found that, on average, people worldwide spend almost two-and-a-half hours on social media each day, and in the United States specifically, it is estimated that people spend upwards of a thousand hours on social media per year.[9] Therefore, if one wants to market journal content, it only makes sense to do it where people spend a good portion of their time.

To illustrate that point, consider Figure 5.1, which shows the number of article downloads for *TRSE* from 2015 to 2021. In 2016, the journal began promoting articles on both Facebook and Twitter, and as one can see from the graph, the number of downloads increased consistently from fewer than 30,000 downloads in 2016 to over 100,000 downloads in 2021. Correlation, of course, does not imply causation, and there were likely other factors at play (e.g., *TRSE* being admitted into the ESCI and, subsequently, the SSCI), but

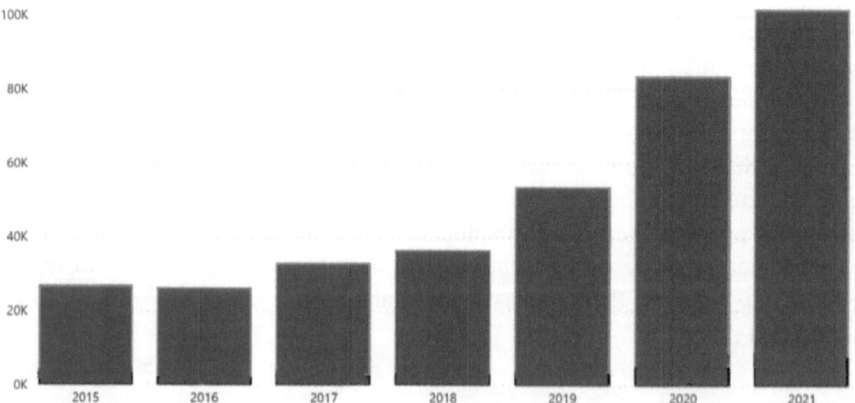

Figure 5.1. Annual TRSE Downloads 2015–2021

it is hard to argue that social media did not have at least some impact in the visibility of the journal over that six-year span.

It is best practice to create social media accounts specifically for the journal, as opposed to using the editor's personal accounts. Doing so encourages a wider audience for journal content and maintains consistency when there is a change in editorship. It is essential that editors publicize the journal accounts and recruit as many initial followers as possible. Doing so will help the journal's social media presence grow over time as the various algorithms are influenced by the number of times people like or share/retweet content.

One way to ease the burden of social media posting is to have authors do some of the work. For example, upon a manuscript's acceptance, all *TRSE* authors receive an email inviting them to submit the following:

- A 100-word summary of the article designed to accompany an initial Facebook post about the article
- A 25-word summary of the article designed for subsequent Facebook posts
- A 250-character summary of the article designed specifically for Twitter
- One or two short quotations from the article that can be used for Facebook or Twitter posts

Typically, authors comply with this request. It provides them with an opportunity to frame their work in the way they see fit, and it takes some of the aesthetic decision-making off the editor. Of course, if authors fail to submit this information, then editors are on the hook for deciding what content to publish online.

The best time to advertise articles is when they first appear online (see next section about ahead-of-print articles) or when an issue is published online. One strategy is to spend a week highlighting each article. A sample schedule might be to post an initial "new article" announcement on Monday, a summary of the article on Tuesday, and then direct quotations from the article on Wednesday and Thursday. Other hints for maximizing a journal's reach on social media include:

- Post at times that are optimal for as many time zones as possible.
- Always include a link to the article in the post; whenever possible use the doi link, which will provide direct navigation to the article online.
- Whenever possible, tag authors, organizations, and/or institutions on the post; it increases the likelihood of shares/retweets.
- Posts on Fridays, Saturdays, and Sundays are typically not viewed as much as posts that occur Monday through Thursday.

- Use Facebook scheduler and/or a program like TweetDeck to schedule posts days, weeks, or months in advance.

Beyond the posts that occur when new articles/issues are released, there are other ways in which editors can utilize social media. For example, if an article published in the journal receives an award, making note of that achievement would be prudent. Similarly, if an article is mentioned in a mainstream news outlet or if a current event is relevant to content published in the journal, that is an optimal time to highlight those respective articles. Other efforts can include posting profiles of editorial team/board members or inviting members of the field to nominate their favorite articles from the journal that could then be highlighted on social media.

Finally, an adage about fishing states that one must go where the fish are; one cannot expect them to come to you. The same applies to any type of marketing efforts. It is important to stay abreast of emerging technology. Facebook, Twitter, and Instagram may be the most effective social media platforms for promoting scholarly activities today, but as the professoriate skews younger, more editors may need to embrace TikTok or whatever platform emerges next.

Ahead-of-Print Articles

It is not uncommon for journals to develop a backlog of accepted content. In the past, that content would have to remain unread for months or, in some cases, years. However, the advent of electronic publishing has allowed journals to publish accepted content online ahead of print. Although these articles are not the version of record, they have a distinct Digital Object Identifier number and can be downloaded and cited, which can contribute to a journal's impact metrics. These ahead-of-print articles are especially important for journals that publish quarterly or biannually.

Open/Free Access Articles

One of the greatest impediments to making journal content accessible is the cost associated with journals being housed within publishing companies. Although many universities purchase bundled subscriptions with publishing companies that include most, if not all, of their respective journals, there are still many scholars who may seek to access an article only to find a paywall instead. Therefore, eliminating that cost can significantly increase downloads and, likely, citations.

There are two terms that most publishing companies use when discussing the removal of paywalls. The first is open access, which is when an author pays a fee to make their work freely accessible in perpetuity. This fee typically ranges in the thousands of dollars, so it is not a feasible option for many authors. However, authors sometimes are able to use grant money to make their work open access, and it is worth encouraging all authors to consider ponying up the money because open access articles receive significantly more downloads than articles behind a paywall. For example, as of this writing, the top four most downloaded *TRSE* articles (and six of the top ten) are open access.

Free access articles are those that are normally behind paywalls but are made freely accessible for short periods of time. Articles are typically made free access as part of a campaign by the publisher to generate downloads and/or publicize specific journals. Oftentimes, the publisher seeks editorial input on which articles should be made free access. These free access articles are then made part of mass email marketing campaigns.

Publishers are often willing to make articles free access upon request. If, say, an article receives an award or is relevant to a high-profile current event, it would be prudent to request that it be made free access. At that point, editors can promote the work on social media. Publishers may also allow journals to publish "virtual issues" of previously published, free access content around a certain theme. As with open access articles, those articles selected for free access campaigns or virtual issues typically generate more downloads than articles hidden behind paywalls.

Other Efforts

Beyond social media and free access campaigns, efforts to promote journals will vary depending on the scope of the journal and the field it represents. As already noted, having research published in a journal cited by mainstream publications is a great way for journal content to reach the masses. However, most newspaper editors, magazine columnists, or blog authors are either unaware of the content academic journals publish or unable to access it due to paywalls. Therefore, one thing that editors can do is be proactive and contact mainstream publications with potential articles of interest.

For example, *TRSE* articles would be of interest to newspapers, magazines, or websites that publish content about education. As such, I have made contacts over the years with editors and columnists from outlets such as *HuffPost* and *Teaching Tolerance*. After issues are published, I often send them an email with the table of contents, and if they express interest in an article, I send them a copy. There is no guarantee that they will use the article in their reporting, but it has happened a few times over the years.

Another venture that *TRSE* has undertaken is a partnership with Visions of Education, which is a podcast hosted by Daniel Krutka, a professor of education at the University of North Texas, and Michael Milton, a high school teacher in Massachusetts.[10] Every *TRSE* author receives an invitation to record a Visions of Education episode in which they are encouraged to talk about their article in accessible language designed for practitioners. These podcasts are then marketed to practitioners and teacher educators, which helps bridge the gap between research and practice that often plagues academia.

TRSE's most recent venture is a YouTube channel, which is also designed to bridge the research and practice divide. Authors are invited to film a short (10–15 minute) video that explains their research in a way that would be useful to practitioners. These videos are designed to be used with preservice teachers, practicing educators, or anyone else who may not be able to access *TRSE* content due to publisher paywalls.

Will this type of marketing lead to a greater number of citations or even downloads? Maybe not. However, if we think about academic publishing as more than just accumulating lines on a vita for promotion and tenure, then we should want our scholarship to have an impact beyond the ivory tower. Making journal content accessible to as many people as possible not only can improve metrics, but it also can help democratize knowledge, which should be a goal of academia writ large.

IMPLICATIONS FOR AUTHORS

How much should authors prioritize journal metrics when determining where to submit their work? Unfortunately, there is not a clear answer to that question. Junior faculty should seek guidance from mentors about how metrics like impact factors or CiteScores are weighed in promotion and tenure decisions. Although more colleges and universities are placing an emphasis on such metrics, oftentimes just noting that a journal has an official impact factor or CiteScore is enough; it may not actually matter how well the journal performs on the respective metric. Having an impact factor or CiteScore indicates that the journal is a legitimate publication that has been vetted by external sources.

Outside of promotion and tenure considerations, there is no need for authors to obsess over journal metrics. Certainly, journals with official metrics often have more visibility, and a journal that performs well on various metrics may indicate that articles published in that journal are more likely to be read and cited than lower performing journals. So, when multiple journals seem like they could be good fits for one's work, it makes sense to go with the one with the best metrics.

However, "chasing metrics" is not a good publication strategy. It is not worth submitting one's work to a journal that is likely not a good fit simply because it performs well on various metrics. Doing so is an invitation for desk rejects or months wasted on external peer review. Remember, many quality journals either do not have official journal metrics or may not perform particularly well on them. Therefore, while journal metrics may be part of one's process for determining where to submit, it should not be the primary consideration.

Like editors, authors should prioritize the visibility of their work. If certain journals have a reputation for promoting authors' work, then that should weigh heavily on the choice of where to submit. With so many journals competing for readers' attention, even articles published in top-tier journals can languish without many downloads or citations if they are not adequately promoted.

It is worth doing research prior to submission on a journal's social media presence, as well as any other types of marketing they offer for authors. If one is fortunate to get their work published in a journal, and the journal offers opportunities to participate in efforts to market the article, definitely take them up on it! In addition to likely increasing the number of people who interact with the published article, these additional activities (e.g., participating on a podcast) look good on one's vita.

Regardless of what a journal may do in terms of publicizing articles, authors are also encouraged to promote their work within their own social media networks and other online platforms. Self-promotion is, for better or worse, part of contemporary academia. Many people may be uncomfortable with promoting their own work—and certainly, some people go overboard—but doing things like sharing the complementary downloads of articles that publishers often give has become an accepted practice within academic circles. As the old saying goes, sometimes people have to be their own best advocate.

NOTES

1. For example, *TRSE* follows the style guide of the American Psychological Association, which states that both Black and White should be capitalized. However, many authors prefer to keep White in lowercase as a way of pushing back against racial hierarchies in society. In those cases, I ask authors to include an endnote explaining their reasoning for leaving White in lowercase.

2. For a sampling of critiques related to the use of impact factors in scholarly decision-making, see "San Francisco Declaration on Research Assessment," Declaration on Research Assessment, accessed June 24, 2022, https://sfdora.org/read/; Michael H. MacRoberts and Barbara R. MacRoberts, "The Mismeasure of Science: Citation Analysis," *Journal of the Association for Information Science and Technology* 69, no. 3 (2018): 474–82, https://doi.org/10.1002/asi.23970; Paul Smeyers and

Nicholas C. Burbules, "How to Improve Your Impact Factor: Questioning the Quantification of Academic Quality," *Journal of Philosophy of Education* 45, no. 1 (2011): 1–17, https://doi.org/10.1111/j.1467-9752.2011.00787.x.

3. "Web of Science Journal Evaluation Process and Selection Criteria," Clarivate, accessed June 23, 2022, https://clarivate.com/products/scientific-and-academic-research/research-discovery-and-workflow-solutions/web-of-science/core-collection/editorial-selection-process/editorial-selection-process/.

4. The Web of Science, formerly known as the Web of Knowledge, is a platform that provides citation data across multiple databases. The Web of Science is currently owned by Clarivate.

5. It is worth noting that while journals in the ESCI do not have an official impact factor, they do, however, contribute to other journals' impact factors. In other words, if an ESCI journal cites a journal in the SCIE, SSCI, or AHCI, it will positively affect the indexed journal's impact factor.

6. Yunlong Cao et al., "Omicron Escapes the Majority of Existing SARS-CoV-2 Neutralizing Antibodies," *Nature* 602 (2022): 657–663, https://doi.org/10.1038/s41586-021-04385-3.

7. "Scopus Content Coverage Guide," Elsevier, last modified 2020, https://www.elsevier.com/__data/assets/pdf_file/0007/69451/Scopus_ContentCoverage_Guide_WEB.pdf.

8. The formula can be found at "Description of SCImago Journal Rank Indicator," SCImago Research Group, last modified 2007, https://www.scimagojr.com/SCImagoJournalRank.pdf.

9. Katharina Buchholz, "Which Countries Spend the Most Time on Social Media?," World Economic Forum, last modified April 29, 2022, https://www.weforum.org/agenda/2022/04/social-media-internet-connectivity/; Peter Suciu, "Americans Spent On Average More Than 1,300 Hours on Social Media Last Year," Forbes, last modified June 24, 2021, https://www.forbes.com/sites/petersuciu/2021/06/24/americans-spent-more-than-1300-hours-on-social-media/?sh=7a5371c52547.

10. The Visions of Education podcast can be found at https://visionsofed.com/podcast/.

Afterword

As this book has shown, journal editing is a complex endeavor that, when done correctly, can be rewarding for both editors and their respective scholarly fields. Yet, the future of journal editing is uncertain. For decades, the fundamentals of editing and publishing in academic journals has remained the same, even as technology made the process more efficient. Recent years, however, have seen changes that suggest fundamental shifts in journal editing may be coming.

Perhaps the most significant change is the fact that academic journal publishing has become a lucrative business for a handful of global publishing companies. For decades, most journals were published by organizations or societies, which severely limited the scope of their research. Without question, the advent of global publishing companies significantly expanded the reach of journals, but at the same time, it turned academic publishing into a multimillion-dollar industry that is built upon the largely free labor of scholars.

It takes minimal scrolling through academic Twitter accounts to find scholars pushing back against this commodification of scholarly knowledge. Consider, for example, this tweet from a *doctoral student* pushing back against the lack of compensation for external reviewers:

> Got a review request today and sent them my fee schedule back - $1,000 flat fee + $350/hour - and got nasty email in reply. Sorry I know what I'm worth (@ billkakenmaster, June 5, 2022)

It is unclear whether this tweet was made in jest, but it sparked a debate about the nature of peer review and the ethics of academic publishing. Many journal editors responded by empathizing with the premise of the tweet but also noting that finding external reviewers has become more difficult and that maintaining expedient external review times for all requires that everyone does their fair share of reviewing.

What I found interesting about that tweet exchange was the number of journal editors who professed having difficulty consistently finding reviewers. One editor, for example, tweeted that she went through 17 potential reviewers for a recently submitted manuscript before the requisite number agreed. Yet, in my nearly decade serving as either editor or associate editor of *TRSE*, I have never really had that problem. Of course, reviewers decline on occasion, and some manuscripts are more difficult to find reviewers for than others, but generally, people agree to review.

There may be a number of reasons why people are more willing to review for *TRSE* than what seemingly occurs in other journals. Being the top journal in its field likely helps, as does the fact that *TRSE* is the official journal of a well-known organization. However, scholars in social studies education are just as burdened as those in other fields, and I have certainly heard rumblings about the lack of monetary compensation for service to the field at our annual conferences.

So, what might explain the difference between my experience and what is seemingly widespread among other scholarly journals? I have no data to support this theory, but I like to think that it is because my reviewers—either through their experiences as *TRSE* authors or reviewers or via word of mouth from others—recognize that if they devote their labor to the journal, they know that the editorial process will be thorough, fair, and worth their time.

I also believe authors acknowledge editorial effort, which is why I have had few negative interactions following reject decisions. I am sure many authors have been disappointed, and likely several have vehemently disagreed with my interpretation of their work or willingness to side with a critical reviewer. However, they can see from the detailed and thoughtful editorial decision letter that I try to provide to each author that the decision was not made hastily.

If there is a theme that runs through this book, it is that the process of journal editing should be guided by an ethic of caring. A caring disposition does not mean that editors cannot or should not reject manuscripts or make difficult decisions. Rather, it means that editors never lose sight of the fact that academic publishing is a challenging endeavor that is inherently designed to ensure that more people fail than succeed.

Being a good editor takes a great deal of time and energy—time and energy that often go unnoticed. The reward is that it leads to an editing process that goes beyond filling pages of a journal. Serving as editor of *TRSE* has been one of the highlights of my career. Seeing how the journal has shaped the field and knowing that I had a hand in that transformation means more to me than any of the articles I have published myself. That feeling may only be rivaled by sharing in the excitement of a young scholar who has just found out that their work has been accepted to a top-tier journal for the first time.

Those postdecision emails—along with the ones from scholars whose work was rejected but who sincerely appreciate the feedback—provide the motivation to continue putting forth that level of time and energy. It is my hope that this book provides potential editors with the foundation that they need to be successful, so that they can focus more on that ethic of caring. Academia can be a harsh, isolating environment, but it does not have to be that way. Journal editors are in a unique position to change the culture of scholarly publishing from that of a Reviewer 2 to one that is humanizing and affirming of scholars' work, which should be the goal of scholarly publishing moving forward.

Appendix A

Manuscripts Focusing on Race Submitted to TRSE from July 1, 2016, to December 31, 2021

Note 1: Manuscripts were determined to focus on race if they meet one or more of the following conditions:

- The main topic of the manuscript was about the experiences of BIPOC students, teachers, or preservice teachers.
- The topic of the manuscript was about racism, whiteness, or settler colonialism.
- The topic of the manuscript was about the representation of BIPOC individuals/groups in textbooks, state curriculum standards, or other curricular material.

Note 2: Authors and reviewers are identified as BIPOC or White. For the reviewers, the font indicates their publication recommendation. Words in **bold** indicate a decision of "accept" or "accept, pending revision"; words in *italics* indicate a decision of "reject, encourage resubmission"; and words underlined indicate a decision of "reject." In the event that the race of an author or reviewer is not known, the word "unknown" is given.

Note 3: For the sake of space and redundancy, only the initial submission that was sent out for external review is listed. The only exception is for manuscript UTRS-2016–0099; that manuscript was a revision of a manuscript previously submitted before July 1, 2016, and had received a "reject, encourage resubmission" decision. If a manuscript was given a "reject, encourage resubmission" decision, it is noted whether the manuscript was eventually published.

Manuscript Identification Number	First Author's Race	Reviewers' Race	Editorial Decision
UTRS-2016–0071	BIPOC	**BIPOC**, *BIPOC*, **BIPOC**	Reject, Encourage Resubmission (eventually published)
UTRS-2016–0080	Unknown	*White*, **BIPOC**, *BIPOC*	Reject, Encourage Resubmission (rejected after resubmission)
UTRS-2016–0081	BIPOC	**White**, <u>White</u>, *White*	Reject
UTRS-2016–0082	White	**BIPOC**, **BIPOC**, *BIPOC*, *BIPOC*	Reject, Encourage Resubmission (eventually published)
UTRS-2016–0087	BIPOC	<u>BIPOC</u>, <u>White</u>, **BIPOC**, <u>BIPOC</u>	Reject
UTRS-2016–0093	White	*White*, *White*, *BIPOC*	Reject
UTRS-2016–0099	BIPOC	*White*, **White**, **BIPOC**	Accept, Pending Revision (revision of a previously submitted manuscript)
UTRS-2016–0116	White	*White*, *White*, *BIPOC*	Reject
UTRS-2016–0117	Unknown	*White*, **White**, **Unknown**	Reject, Encourage Resubmission (eventually published)
UTRS-2017–0044	White	*White*, **White**, *BIPOC*	Reject, Encourage Resubmission (eventually published)
UTRS-2017–0063	White	*White*, *BIPOC*, *BIPOC*	Reject
UTRS-2017–0083	BIPOC	**BIPOC**, *White*, *BIPOC*	Reject, Encourage Resubmission (eventually published)
UTRS-2017–0122	White	<u>White</u>, **White**, *BIPOC*, **BIPOC**	Reject, Encourage Resubmission (eventually published)
UTRS-2017–0123	Unknown	*BIPOC*, *White*, <u>BIPOC</u>	Reject, Encourage Resubmission (did not submit revision)
UTRS-2018–0006	BIPOC	*White*, **BIPOC,** *White*	Reject
UTRS-2018–0034	White	*BIPOC*, <u>*BIPOC*</u>, *BIPOC*	Reject, Encourage Resubmission (eventually published)
UTRS-2018–0035	BIPOC	<u>White</u>, *White*, **BIPOC**	Reject, Encourage Resubmission (eventually published)
UTRS-2018–0064	White	*White*, *BIPOC*, *White*	Reject, Encourage Resubmission (rejected after resubmission)
UTRS-2018–0067	White	*White*, **White,** **BIPOC**	Accept, Pending Revisions
UTRS-2018–0069	White	<u>White</u>, s, *BIPOC*	Reject

UTRS-2018–0078	BIPOC	**White**, *BIPOC*, **BIPOC**	Reject, Encourage Resubmission (eventually published)
UTRS-2018–0090	White	*White*, **White**, *White*	Reject, Encourage Resubmission (eventually published)
UTRS-2019–0003	White	*White, BIPOC,* **White**	Reject, Encourage Resubmission (eventually published)
UTRS-2019–0012	BIPOC	**White**, *White, White*	Reject, Encourage Resubmission (eventually published)
UTRS-2019–0052	White	*White, BIPOC, BIPOC*	Reject, Encourage Resubmission (eventually published)
UTRS-2019–0057	White	*White, BIPOC,* <u>BIPOC</u>	Reject, Encourage Resubmission (rejected after resubmission)
UTRS-2019–0062	BIPOC	<u>BIPOC</u>, *BIPOC,* **BIPOC**	Reject, Encourage Resubmission (eventually published)
UTRS-2019–0067	White	<u>White</u>, *White, White,* <u>White</u>	Reject
UTRS-2019–0069	White	*White*, **White**, **BIPOC**	Reject, Encourage Resubmission (eventually published)
UTRS-2019–0077	BIPOC	**BIPOC**, <u>White</u>, **White**	Reject, Encourage Resubmission (rejected after resubmission)
UTRS-2019–0081	BIPOC	*White*, <u>BIPOC</u>, <u>White</u>	Reject
UTRS-2019–0140	White	*White*, **White**, *White*	Reject, Encourage Resubmission (eventually published)
UTRS-2020–0048	BIPOC	**BIPOC**, *BIPOC,* **BIPOC**, *BIPOC*	Reject, Encourage Resubmission (eventually published)
UTRS-2020–0051	White	*BIPOC,* <u>White</u>, *White*	Reject, Encourage Resubmission (rejected after resubmission)
UTRS-2020–0056	White	*BIPOC, BIPOC,* **BIPOC**	Reject, Encourage Resubmission (rejected after resubmission)
UTRS-2020–0066	White	<u>BIPOC</u>, <u>White</u>, *White*	Reject
UTRS-2020–0074	BIPOC	*BIPOC,* <u>BIPOC</u>	Reject
UTRS-2020–0098	BIPOC	*White, White, White, Unknown*	Reject, Encourage Resubmission (eventually published)
UTRS-2020–0118	Unknown	**BIPOC**, *White,* **BIPOC**	Reject, Encourage Resubmission (rejected after resubmission)
UTRS-2020–0135	Unknown	<u>BIPOC</u>, *BIPOC, White*	Reject
UTRS-2020–0185	BIPOC	<u>BIPOC</u>, *BIPOC, BIPOC, BIPOC*	Reject, Encourage Resubmission (eventually published)
UTRS-2021–0010	BIPOC	<u>White</u>, *BIPOC, White*	Reject

UTRS-2021–0018	BIPOC	**Unknown**, **White**, *White*, **Unknown**	Accept, Pending Revisions
UTRS-2021–0030	White	<u>BIPOC</u>, <u>White</u>, <u>BIPOC</u>	Reject
UTRS-2021–0039	BIPOC	**BIPOC**, *BIPOC*, <u>BIPOC</u>	Reject, Encourage Resubmission (eventually published)
UTRS-2021–0097	BIPOC	*BIPOC, BIPOC, White*	Reject, Encourage Resubmission (resubmission never submitted)
UTRS-2021–0117	White	<u>White</u>, *White, White*	Reject, Encourage Resubmission (resubmission never submitted)
UTRS-2021–0134	White	*White, White,* <u>White</u>	Reject, Encourage Resubmission (eventually published)
UTRS-2021–0135	BIPOC	<u>BIPOC</u>, *White*	Reject
UTRS-2021–0141	BIPOC	*BIPOC, White*	Reject, Encourage Resubmission (eventually published)
UTRS-2021–0158	BIPOC	*White,* **BIPOC**, *White, BIPOC*	Reject, Encourage Resubmission (eventually published)

Appendix B

Sample Decision Letter 1

Dr. Jon Wargo
Boston College
July 22, 2020

Dear Jon,

Thank you for your submission to *Theory & Research in Social Education* entitled, "'Sound' Civics, Heard Histories: A Telling Case of Young Children Mobilizing Digital Media to Write (Right) Injustice." I have now received feedback from three reviewers: R1 recommended "reject, encourage resubmission"; R3 recommended "reject, encourage resubmission"; and R4 recommended "accept, pending revision." (R2 was a doctoral student participating in our doctoral reviewer mentorship program. His/Her review was not used in my assessment of your manuscript; however, I have included his/her comments for you to use as you see fit.)

In addition to carefully considering the reviewers' comments, I have also conducted a close read of your work. As someone with a seven-year-old daughter who loves Roblox, I enjoyed reading about how Gordy and Kevin participated in this project. I also believe that the study design was novel, and given the dearth of articles on technology and, in particular, making in the social studies literature, I believe this manuscript has the potential to be of interest to *TRSE* readers. That said, the manuscript needs significant revisions related to organization and theorization before it could be considered for publication in *TRSE*.

Therefore, my editorial decision is to reject the current version of the manuscript; however, I would encourage you to revise and resubmit the manuscript back to *TRSE* if you believe you can adequately address the concerns raised by the reviewers and the issues I raise in this letter. This revision would undergo another round of external review, and acceptance is not guaranteed.

The reviewers have provided valuable feedback, both in terms of identifying weaknesses in the manuscript as well as offering suggestions for improving the manuscript. I recommend that you address as many of their concerns as possible should you decide to revise and resubmit to *TRSE*. I will not reiterate all of their concerns here; rather, I will attempt to synthesize their comments along with my own reading of the manuscript and offer suggestions for revisions.

Overarching Issue:

- There is an overarching issue that affects the overall coherence of the manuscript, which is that this manuscript comes from a larger study. That in itself is not a problem; a good dissertation, for example, will typically yield multiple articles. However, culling individual articles out of a larger study is a skill, and if you don't do it carefully, the individual articles get muddled.

Too often in this manuscript, you write as if the readers are familiar with that larger study. When you carve manuscripts from a larger study, you have to make sure that you are providing sufficient detail and organizing the manuscript so that it can stand on its own. Throughout this manuscript, you occasionally leave out key details (e.g., how you collected data from the teachers) and include information that is relevant to the larger study but not to this specific paper (e.g., the names of the schools in Michigan and Northeast Massachusetts).

I have always found the idea of a straight line helpful. You should be able to draw a straight line from your introduction through your literature review, theoretical framework, methods, findings, and discussion. That straight line should be focused on the data that you present in the manuscript. If anything falls outside of that straight line, get rid of it. What is left on the straight line should build on each other so that you end up telling a coherent story about what is presented in *this manuscript*, not necessarily the larger study.

Introduction:

- The vignettes were interesting, but what is missing from the introduction is a "big picture" justification of the study. As you note in the manuscript, there has not been much done on making in the social studies literature, so I think a short explanation of what making is and why it is important is needed here.
- I do not believe that your third research question is actually a research question; it is not something that you can necessarily "answer" with your

findings. Rather, it sounds like an analytical question that you could explore in the discussion section of the manuscript.

- Minor issue, but you need a citation for the *Hey Wall!* book.

Literature Review/Theoretical Framework:

- This section needs quite a bit of work. It is clear that you are well versed in the literature; however, I agree with the reviewers that you do not flesh out this literature with enough depth. For example, you cover the civic education of young children in just two paragraphs and you don't elaborate on any of the studies that you cite. Being able to unpack the literature is important because it will help you make a case in the discussion for how your study advances the field. I also agree with R1 that in addition to unpacking each of the areas that comprise the literature review, you need to do a better job of explaining how they are all integrated. Right now, you kind of jump between topics, and it is difficult to see how everything works together.
- I agree with R4 that the manuscript is undertheorized with respect to democratic/civic education. There exists quite a bit of literature on how young children develop civic understandings and work with each other to discuss and "solve" civic issues. Jenn Hauver's work, which you cite, really speaks to this aspect of your study, and I would encourage you to unpack her work a bit more. I would also look at work by Stephanie Serriere and Dana Mitra as a starting point.
- In the section on making and young children's digital design, you are correct that scant attention has been paid to examining making with children under 9 years old, which makes describing what research that has been done even more important. I would encourage you to unpack the Marsh et al. and Peppler et al. studies in greater depth, as well as your previous work, to the extent you can do so while maintaining blind review (FYI—I think that citation should be Author & Colleague, 2020a, not 2000a).
- Although it is not necessarily making in the same sense that you are using it in this study, I think an article published a couple of years ago that used GIS with students to engage in "citizen mapping" could be of use to you here:

    Schlemper, M. B., Stewart, V. C., Shetty, S., & Czajkowski, K. (2018). Including Students' Geographies in Geography Education: Spatial Narratives, Citizen Mapping, and Social Justice. *Theory & Research in Social Education, 46*(4), 603–641. https://doi.org/10.1080/00933104.2018.1427164

- It is unclear what the theoretical framework driving the study is. My guess is that it is critical literacy. Is that the case? If so, then I think you need to clearly label it as such, and again, you need to unpack it in much greater depth. Also, if critical literacy is the theoretical framework, then the section on speculative design seems out of place. Is it part of the theoretical framework? Or is it part of the literature review on making? In short, there is some reorganization that needs to take place here.
- I agree with R1 and R3 that sound is undertheorized in this manuscript, particularly given its importance to the study. I would also encourage you to consider R1's suggestion about incorporating research on sound-scapes/sound making, either within the section on speculative design or as its own section.
- On page 7, you bring up Kevin and Gordy, but you have not introduced them as the focal students in the study yet.

Methods:

- As I noted above, I think this study is quite innovative. However, there are many aspects of the study that need clarification:
  - How was Williams chosen for participation in MakEY? Did the school have prior experience with making? Similarly, how were Ms. Steele and Ms. Flowers chosen? Did they have experience with making?
  - I agree with R1 that you need to explain how you went from 53 to 23 to 2 students. Why Kevin and Gordy? Later in the manuscript, you note that their project was not necessarily the most interesting or even the best example of digital dexterity or civic competence. So, why choose them?
  - You need to provide more information about Kevin and Gordy in this section. It isn't until the findings that we find out their age and race. (I would have a subsection just on participants.)
  - It is clear that you collected data from the teachers as well; how were those data collected? Interviews?
  - Please include a protocol for your design interviews as an appendix. It is also not clear when those interviews occurred (e.g., at the end of the study? The middle?). The transcripts from Kevin and Gordy in the findings section seem like they occurred soon after each part of the project occurred. Please clarify.
  - In your data analysis section, you talk about your procedures in general terms. I think it would help the reader if you could give some examples of how you coded the data.

- I agree with R3 that you need a positionality statement within the methods section. I would also add that you need to include a limitations section as well.

Findings:

- The findings are interesting, and I agree with R4 that the transcripts that you provide are good. That said, I agree with R3 that at times, the findings came across as your interpretations rather than a thick description of the data. For example, pages 14–16 almost seem like a description of context, as opposed to findings that answer your research questions. You do not really get to Kevin and Gordy's project until page 17. If the units of analysis are Kevin and Gordy, the findings section should be primarily about them.
- At some points, more context is needed. For example, at the top of page 23, that section just kind of ends. We find out that people in Ramsay Park protested about something, but it seems to come out of the blue.
- At points, it became difficult to understand the findings section due to the number of specific technological applications (e.g., Kinex) and seven-year-old lingo (e.g., Stikbot) that you throw out there. Some endnotes that offer explanation for what these things are would be helpful.

Discussion:

- This section is probably the one that needs the most work. Right now, you don't really get at the "so what" aspect of the study. I agree with R4 that you do a pretty good job with critical literacy, but the democratic element (which is what most *TRSE* readers are likely going to care about) is not really analyzed here. How does this manuscript move the field forward in new or significant ways? Yes, the fact that the students engaged in a civic education making project is unique to the field, but that alone is not sufficient. What did this making activity illuminate about the civic education of young kids?

I think the way you can really answer that question is to reincorporate your literature review and theoretical framework into your analysis. By doing so, you can show how your study addresses gaps in the literature, and it would allow you to take a more critical look at your findings. I agree with R1 that you need to acknowledge and attempt to explain the tensions that occurred with Kevin and Gordy within the context of this project. Being able to situate those tensions within critical literacy and the research on civic education will help you do that.

Minor Issues:

- *TRSE* has recently moved to the 7th edition of the APA handbook. As a result, your revised manuscript will need to conform to the 7th edition, particularly with respect to your references and citations. Below my signature line in this letter, I have included a "cheat sheet" that explains the main differences between the 6th and 7th editions.
- Please be consistent on the spelling of Ms. Flowers's name. Sometimes it is Ms. Flowers and other times it is Ms. Flower.
- APA stipulates that references to previously published work should be written in either the past tense or the present perfect tense, *not the present tense*. See page 118 in the APA Manual, 7th edition. You need to make this change throughout the manuscript.
- APA stipulates that Black and White be capitalized. If you have ideological reasons for putting one or both in lowercase, please explain your reasoning in an endnote.
- Please include your appendices as part of the main document, not as separate files in Manuscript Central.
- Please do not embed your figures at the end of the main document. Instead upload them as separate files (like you already did). Include the captions for the figures either when you upload them into Manuscript Central or include them in the main document after you put "Insert Figure X Here."

I understand that the decision not to publish your work at this time is disappointing. I also appreciate that I (and the reviewers) may have misunderstood aspects of the manuscript, but oftentimes any such misunderstandings also point to areas that need further clarification.

I am optimistic that you can address the concerns articulated in this letter. If so, I hope that you will consider revising the manuscript and resubmitting it to *TRSE*. I also hope that you find both my comments and the reviewers' comments helpful as you undertake your revision. You should feel free to disagree with me or the reviewers, but I ask that you help me understand your thinking. If you decide to resubmit, please include a *blinded* letter that explains how you responded to my suggestions and the suggestions made by the reviewers. Your revision will be sent out for another round of external review, and this letter will be shared with the reviewers. Please be aware that attention to the reviewers' comments enhances but does not guarantee acceptance.

I certainly hope that you decide to submit a revision to *TRSE*, but of course, you are free to submit the manuscript elsewhere at this time if you so choose.

Please let me know if I can be of any help as you work through your revisions.

Appendix C

Sample Decision Letter 2

Dr. Aaron Bodle
James Madison University
November 12, 2021

Dear Dr. Bodle,

Thank you for your submission to *Theory & Research in Social Education* entitled, "Lessons Learned and Unlearned in a Critical Place-based Elementary Social Studies Course." I have now received feedback from three reviewers: R1 recommended "reject, encourage resubmission"; R2 recommended "reject, encourage resubmission"; and R3 recommended "reject."

In addition to carefully considering the reviewers' comments, I have also conducted a close read of your work. It is an innovative study and one that would be of interest to *TRSE* readers. In short, there is a ton of potential here. That said, there are significant issues related to the manuscript's framing, organization, and description of methods that need revising before this manuscript could be considered for publication.

Therefore, my editorial decision is to reject the current version of the manuscript; however, I would encourage you to revise and resubmit the manuscript back to *TRSE* if you believe you can adequately address the concerns raised by the reviewers and the issues I raise in this letter. This revision would undergo another round of external review, and acceptance is not guaranteed.

The reviewers have provided valuable feedback, both in terms of identifying weaknesses in the manuscript as well as offering suggestions for improving the manuscript. I recommend that you address as many of their concerns as possible should you decide to revise and resubmit to *TRSE*. I will not reiterate all of their concerns here; rather, I will attempt to synthesize their comments along with my own reading of the manuscript and offer suggestions for revisions.

Overarching Issues:

- I think you are trying to do too much in one manuscript. It seems to me that the main focus of this manuscript, at least as defined by the abstract, literature review, and theoretical framework, is understanding how a place-based experience with PSTs can contribute to antiracism pedagogy. I agree with R1 that if you can make that case, this study has the potential to be groundbreaking for the field. However, the findings section covers all sorts of stuff, ranging from how students responded to Madison's legacy of slavery to how archaeology led to students' overall understanding of history to the benefits of experiential learning.

Here is how I suggest that you proceed: Focus only on how the place-based instruction led to students' understanding of race/racism. Save the interdisciplinary connections/experiential learning and its relationship to their understanding of history for another manuscript. Doing so will help streamline the manuscript and allow you to really unpack the implications of place-based historical learning on the goal of teaching for antiracism, which I think would help address R3's concern that this study needs to offer something tangible to readers beyond just a description of a cool pedagogical opportunity.

In making this change, I think you would want to refine your second research question to be something like "In what ways did this place-based experience support their understanding of race/racism?" Similarly, I would consider changing the title so that it acknowledges the importance of race in this study.

- The organization of the manuscript is problematic. For example, you randomly have a section on "Course Context" starting on page 3, but then you launch into a literature review and theoretical framework. You don't return to what you did in the course until the research design.

R3 is correct; a good manuscript can be thought of as having a straight line going through it with each subsequent section relating to the one before it. Assuming you take my advice and focus on place-based learning and race, here is how I would suggest that the manuscript be organized:

Introduction (i.e., general overview, research questions) → Literature Review (i.e., place-based learning in social studies teacher education, pedagogy of historical sites, race in elementary preservice teacher education) → Theoretical Framework (i.e., critical pedagogy of place, antiracist pedagogy) → Study context (i.e., a description of Montpelier, what students did in the course) → Methods (i.e., participants, data collection, data analysis, limitations) → Findings → Discussion

- What seems to be completely missing from this manuscript, as currently written, is the study context section. We find out bits and pieces about Montpelier and what students were supposed to do there in the findings section, but that information needs to be foregrounded. You need to give a general description of what visitors will find when they visit Montpelier. For example, it does not appear to overly glorify Madison (i.e., they do not hide his legacy of slavery). Then, you need to fully explain what you had students do on site. How often were they there? What were the assignments that were given? (for example, we find out that they have to do an IDM; how did that relate to what they learned at Montpelier?).

Those are the overarching issues that seem to affect the entire manuscript. In the remainder of the letter, I will provide suggestions section by section:

Abstract:

- Both R1 and R2 raised concerns about the first sentence, so you either need to revise or delete (I would suggest the latter—just FYI, APA guidelines say no citations in an abstract). Also, an abstract is designed to give a summary of the study, not project future goals, etc. Therefore, your final sentence is not appropriate for an abstract and would be better suited as part of the discussion.

Introduction:

- The final paragraph of the introduction is out of place. It seems like it would better fit after the sentence that starts with "In a racist society." I think it would be more effective if you ended the introduction with your research questions.

Literature Review:

- Overall, I thought the literature review was strong. Just a few minor comments:
  - I agree with R2 that you want to be specific, including in the subheadings, that you are focusing on teacher education, not K-12 education.
  - In the subsection on centering race in social studies [teacher] education, I would encourage you to look at more work by Lisa Buchanan. You cite her 2016 piece that looks at immigration, but she has other articles focusing on how White preservice elementary teachers

struggle with race when learning about the Civil Rights Movement. Here are a couple of relevant citations:

  Buchanan, L. B. (2015). "We make it controversial": Elementary preservice teachers' beliefs about race. *Teacher Education Quarterly, 42*(1), 3–26.

  Buchanan, L. B. (2016). Elementary preservice teachers' navigation of racism and whiteness through inquiry with historical documentary film. *Journal of Social Studies Research, 40*(2), 137–154. https://doi.org/10.1016/j.jssr.2015.06.006.

- The place-based learning subsection is a good example of where R2 noted that you are focusing on elementary students and not PSTs. Has there been research on place-based learning in teacher education? Elementary teacher education specifically? If so, talk about that. If not, that is a good thing to note.
- I think the "Archaeology, Education, and Interdisciplinary Dialogue" section needs to be dropped.

Theoretical Framework:

- I think the two frames that you use are appropriate for this study, but you don't unpack them with any depth. For the critical pedagogy of place, I was surprised not to see Sandra Schmidt's work referenced here. Beyond social studies, there is a whole field of critical geography education that you can draw from.

Similarly, I was surprised not to see more written about antiracist teaching and learning. Certainly, Kendi and Love are relevant to this conversation, but what has been written about antiracist pedagogy in social studies education and teacher education? You have cited a number of the scholars who do this work earlier in the manuscript, but now is the time to really unpack what you mean by antiracism and how it is different from other forms of progressive/justice-oriented instruction.

Methods:

- This is the weakest section of the manuscript. You need to provide WAY more detail about your participants, the data you collected, and your processes of analysis. In fact, I would argue that you need separate subsections for each of those things where you can unpack them fully.
- With respect to the participants, we need to know more about where they were in their programs, what courses they had had building up to this one (i.e., did they have a foundation of antiracist pedagogy or

historical thinking, or was this their first foray into one/both?), and a bit more information about their backgrounds. Also, you note that they were graduate students; what were their undergraduate degrees in?

- With respect to the data collection, well, we pretty much need to know everything. ;) You note that you analyzed the participants' coursework and interview transcripts. What constituted the coursework? How many times did you interview them? Individually or focus groups? What questions did you ask?
- With respect to data analysis, you need to go beyond just generic language about coding. What codes did you use? Where did they come from? (e.g., the literature, your theoretical framework). Give examples of how you coded information. Did you code the data together? Did you engage in aspects of interrater reliability? Member checking?
- You give a nice, brief positionality statement, but you don't talk about how your positionality (as course instructors and as White folks) may have influenced the design of the study and the analysis of the data.
- Finally, I think you need a limitations section in which you talk about the potential limitations of the study and the ability to generalize (or lack thereof). One limitation is obviously the fact that you are researching your own teaching (although that can be strength as well). Another limitation is the fact that only five PSTs agreed to participate. Finally, the fact that you did this study at Montpelier is both a strength and a limitation. It is a strength because it is a great example of a place-based instructional site. It is a limitation because it is extremely specific and most people are not going to have access to something of that magnitude.

Findings:

- The findings are an interesting read, but as I noted above, they try to cover too much ground. Streamline to focus specifically on the place-based and antiracist components. You can remove the other stuff and save it for a different manuscript. Use that space to really unpack the participants' experiences with respect to race.

Discussion:

- I think the discussion will evolve naturally based on the changes that you are making to the manuscript, but you really want to do the following: (1) make a case for the "so-what" aspect of the study. Like R1, I believe that if you can make this connection between place-based pedagogy and antiracist education, that is definitely something significant for the field. However, you want to reincorporate aspects of your literature review and theoretical framework to help make that case; and (2) Draw explicit implications from this research for other social studies teacher education programs. R3 is correct in that you want to be able to make a case that this research is more than just a unique opportunity that your students had but would not necessarily transfer to other contexts. What lessons can other teacher educators who don't have access to something like Montpelier take from this study?

Minor Issues:

- APA stipulates that White and Black be capitalized. If you have ideological reasons for keeping one or both lowercase, please explain in an endnote.
- APA stipulates that references to previously published work should be written in either the past tense or the present perfect tense, *not the present tense*. See page 118 in the APA Manual, 7th edition. You need to make this change throughout the manuscript.
- There were works cited in the text that were not included in the reference list.
- In your reference list, you have doi links for most of the journals that use them, but not all. Also, make sure you use the http://doi.org format and not the DOI: format.

I understand that the decision not to publish your work at this time is disappointing. I also appreciate that I (and the reviewers) may have misunderstood aspects of the manuscript, but oftentimes any such misunderstandings also point to areas that need further clarification.

I am optimistic that you can address the concerns articulated in this letter. If so, I hope that you will consider revising the manuscript and resubmitting it to *TRSE*. I also hope that you find both my comments and the reviewers' comments helpful as you undertake your revision. You should feel free to disagree with me or the reviewers, but I ask that you help me understand your thinking. If you decide to resubmit, please include a *blinded* letter that explains how you responded to my suggestions and the suggestions made by the reviewers. Your revision will be sent out for another round of external review, and this letter will be shared with the reviewers. Please be aware that attention to the reviewers' comments enhances but does not guarantee acceptance.

I certainly hope that you decide to submit a revision to *TRSE*, but of course, you are free to submit the manuscript elsewhere at this time if you so choose.

Please let me know if I can be of any help as you work through your revisions.

Appendix D

Preparing the Manuscript for Publication Checklist

The following are general issues that should be addressed in preparing the manuscript for publication:

- Although quite lucidly written, the manuscript does need another round of editing for grammar, missing words, spelling errors, missed apostrophes, contractions (not to be used in APA 7th), etc. Please also ensure that you use gender-neutral language throughout the manuscript.
- Please add your abstract to your manuscript and add 3–7 keywords after the abstract. See any recent issue of *TRSE* for formatting.
- Third Party Content: This refers to permission lines for figures and tables. Please include permission for reuse / rights holder information for any third-party tables or figures included in your manuscript. Permission to reuse must be obtained from the rights holder prior to publication. If the rights holder has supplied text for this purpose, please use their text. Otherwise, please insert the rights holder's name within the square brackets as follows: © **[rights holder]. Reproduced by permission of [rights holder]**. This information should appear immediately following the table or figure.
- If you want to acknowledge anyone who helped with the study, or gave you substantive feedback during your writing process, now is the time. (Just FYI, APA stipulates that you should not acknowledge reviewers or editors. The exception is if you want to acknowledge a specific idea suggested by a reviewer, in which case you should cite that idea.) Acknowledgments should appear at the end of your manuscript *but before the References section*. Please use the heading (align with left margin): **ACKNOWLEDGMENTS**.

- If your study was funded and you want to acknowledge that funding, you should do so in a short paragraph *following your acknowledgments*. Please use the heading (align with left margin): **FUNDING**.
- You may be writing other articles or publications related to this study. If any are in print or accepted for publication, now is the time to insert them. Be sure to change any Author citations, and insert your work into the References section.
- I really encourage you to check all of your references very carefully. I have not yet checked to see that information such as dates, volume and issue numbers, publication place, and pages numbers were accurate. We all know the frustration of following up on a reference and being directed to the wrong year, page number, etc. So, for all those who will read your work and want to follow up on some of the references, please take an hour or two to check everything very carefully. Scholars interested in your work will appreciate your time.
- Include the Digital Object Identifier (doi) for articles for which this is available. One way to locate a DOI is through your library's databases or by looking on the first page of a publication. You can also use: http://www.crossref.org/guestquery/ to locate the DOI. When you add a DOI to a reference, use the https format (see APA 7th edition).

Bibliography

Anbazhagan, Ram, Hoglah Dasari, and Anita Yadav. "Why Publish Special Issues? An Overview of Wiley's Special Issue Program and an Editor's Experience." The Wiley Network. Last modified December 16, 2019. https://www.wiley.com/network/archive/why-publish-special-issues-an-overview-of-wileys-special-issue-program-and-an-editors-experience.

Aponte-Safe, Gerardo Joel, Ana Carolina Díaz Beltrán, and Rebecca C. Christ. "Aspiring Nepantleras: Conceptualizing Social Studies Education from the Rupture/La Herida Abierta." *Theory & Research in Social Education* 50, no. 1 (2022): 74–100. https://doi.org/10.1080/00933104.2021.2009948.

Avery, Patricia G. "From the Editor." *Theory & Research in Social Education* 41, no. 4 (2013): 581–82. https://doi.org/10.1080/00933104.2013.858579.

Barton, Keith C., and Linda S. Levstik. *Teaching History for the Common Good.* Mahwah: Lawrence Erlbaum Associates, 2004.

Baruch, Yehuda. "Opening the Black Box of Editorship: Editors' Voice." In *Opening the Black Box of Editorship,* edited by Yehuda Baruch, Alison M. Konrad, Herman Aguinis, and William H. Starbuck, 209–22. New York: Palgrave MacMillan, 2008.

Binford, Paul E., and Seth Eisworth. "The Growing Gap: The Origin of *Theory & Research in Social Education.*" *Theory & Research in Social Education* 41, no. 4 (2013): 457–75. https://doi.org/10.1080/00933104.2013.840755.

Brown, D. G. "On Doffing the Mask." *Journal of Academic Ethics* 5, no. 2–4 (2007): 217–19. https://doi.org/10.1007/s10805-007-9034-8.

Brown, Sarah Drake. "Preparing Effective History Teachers: The Assessment Gap." *Journal of Social Studies Research* 37, no. 3 (2013): 167–77. https://doi.org/10.1016/j.jssr.2013.04.005.

Brown, Sarah Drake. "Response to Marchant, Schoenfeldt, and Powell." *Journal of Social Studies Research* 37, no. 3 (2013): 183–84. https://doi.org/10.1016/j.jssr.2013.05.002.

Buchholz, Katharina. "Which Countries Spend the Most Time on Social Media?" World Economic Forum. Last modified April 29, 2022. https://www.weforum.org/agenda/2022/04/social-media-internet-connectivity/.

Burbules, Nicholas C. "Philosophical Reflections on Editing." *Educational Theory,* 54, no. 4 (2014): 317–31. https://doi.org/10.1111/edth.12069.

Clarivate. "Web of Science Journal Evaluation Process and Selection Criteria." Accessed June 24, 2022. https://clarivate.com/products/scientific-and-academic -research/research-discovery-and-workflow-solutions/web-of-science/core -collection/editorial-selection-process/editorial-selection-process/.

Cao, Yunlong, Jing Wang, Fanchong Jian, Tianhe Xiao, Weiliang Song, Ayijiang Yisimayi, Weijin Huang et al. "Omicron Escapes the Majority of Existing SARS-CoV-2 Neutralizing Antibodies." *Nature* 602 (2022): 657–63. https://doi.org /10.1038/s41586-021-04385-3.

Corlett, J. Angelo. "Ethical Issues in Journal Peer-Review." *Journal of Academic Ethics* 2, no. 4 (2005): 355–66. https://doi.org/10.1007/s10805-005-9001-1.

Corlett, J. Angelo. "The Ethics of Academic Journal Editing." *Journal of Academic Ethics* 6, no. 3 (2008): 205–9. https://doi.org/10.1007/s10805-008-9067-7.

Declaration on Research Assessment. "San Francisco Declaration on Research Assessment." Accessed June 24, 2022. https://sfdora.org/read/.

Elsevier. "Scopus Content Coverage Guide." Accessed June 24, 2022. https://www .elsevier.com/__data/assets/pdf_file/0007/69451/Scopus_ContentCoverage_Guide _WEB.pdf.

Endacott, Jason, and Sarah Brooks. "An Updated Theoretical and Practical Model for Promoting Historical Empathy." *Social Studies Research and Practice* 8, no. 1 (2013): 41–58.

Eveleth, Rose. "Academics Write Papers Arguing over How Many People Read (and Cite) Their Papers." Smithsonian Magazine. Last modified March 25, 2014. https: //www.smithsonianmag.com/smart-news/half-academic-studies-are-never-read -more-three-people-180950222/.

Feldman, Daniel C. "Building and Maintaining a Strong Editorial Board and Cadre of Ad Hoc Reviewers." In *Opening the Black Box of Editorship*, edited by Yehuda Baruch, Alison M. Konrad, Herman Aguinis, and William H. Starbuck, 68–74. New York: Palgrave Macmillan, 2008.

Galipeau, James, David Moher, Becky Skidmore, Craig Campbell, Paul Hendry, D. William Cameron, Paul C. Hébert, and Anita Palepu. "Systematic Review of the Effectiveness of Training Programs in Writing for Scholarly Publication, Journal Editing, and Manuscript Peer Review." *Systematic Reviews* 2, no. 1 (2013): 1–7.

Gans, Joshua S., and George B. Shepherd. "How Are the Mighty Fallen: Rejected Classic Articles by Leading Economists." *The Journal of Economic Perspectives* 8, no. 1 (1994): 165–79.

Godlee, Fiona. "Making Reviewers Visible: Openness, Accountability, and Credit." *Journal of the American Medical Association* 287, no. 21 (2002): 2762–65. https: //doi.org/10.1001/jama.287.21.2762.

Henson, Kenneth T. "Writing for Publication: A Shift in Perspective." *Phi Delta Kappan,* 90, no. 10 (2009): 776a–76d. https://doi.org/10.1177%2F003172170909001023.

Huijgen, Tim, Carla van Boxtel, Wim van de Grift, and Paul Holthuis. "Toward Historical Perspective Taking: Students' Reasoning When Contextualizing the Actions of People in the Past." *Theory & Research in Social Education* 45, no. 1 (2017): 110–41. https://doi.org/10.1080/00933104.2016.1208597.

Jackson, Alicia Y., and Lisa A. Mazzei. *Thinking with Theory in Qualitative Research: Viewing Data Across Multiple Perspectives.* New York: Routledge, 2012.

Jago, Arthur G. "Can it Really be True that Half of Academic Papers are Never Read?" The Chronicle of Higher Education. Last modified June 1, 2018. https://www.chronicle.com/article/can-it-really-be-true-that-half-of-academic-papers-are-never-read/.

Journell, Wayne. "From the Editor." *Theory & Research in Social Education* 45, no. 1 (2017): 1–6. https://doi.org/10.1080/00933104.2016.1272328.

Konrad, Alison M. "Knowledge Creation and the Journal Editor's Role." In *Opening the Black Box of Editorship,* edited by Yehuda Baruch, Alison M. Konrad, Herman Aguinis, and William H. Starbuck, 3–15. New York: Palgrave Macmillan, 2008.

Luey, Beth. "The Profession of Journal Editing." *Profession* 2009, no. 1 (2009): 112–18.

MacRoberts, Michael H., and Barbara R. MacRoberts. "The Mismeasure of Science: Citation Analysis." *Journal of the Association for Information Science and Technology* 69, no. 3 (2018): 474–82. https://doi.org/10.1002/asi.23970.

Marchant, Gregory J., Melinda K. Schoenfeldt, and James H. Powell. "A Response to Brown: The role of LAMP in Content and Assessment of Teaching." *Journal of Social Studies Research* 37, no. 3 (2013): 181–82. https://doi.org/10.1016/j.jssr.2013.05.001.

McAfee, R. Preston. "Edifying Editing." *The American Economist* 55, no. 1 (2010): 1–8. https://doi.org/10.1177%2F056943451005500101.

Meho, Lokman I. "The Rise and Rise of Citation Analysis." *Physics World* 20, no. 1 (2007): 32–36.

National Baseball Hall of Fame. "BBWAA election rules." Accessed June 23, 2022. https://baseballhall.org/hall-of-famers/rules/bbwaa-rules-for-election.

Nelson, Jack L., and William B. Stanley. "Critical Studies and Social Education: 40 Years of *TRSE*." *Theory & Research in Social Education* 41, no. 4 (2013): 438–56. https://doi.org/10.1080/00933104.2013.842598.

Posnanski, Joe. *The Baseball 100.* New York: Avid Reader Press, 2021.

Repiso, Rafael, Jesús Segarra-Saavedra, Tatiana Hidalgo-Marí, and Victoria Tur-Viñes. "The Prevalence and Impact of Special Issues in Communications Journals 2015–2019." *Learned Publishing* 34, no. 4 (2021): 593–601. https://doi.org/10.1002/leap.1406.

Roth, Wolff-Michael. "Editorial Power/Authorial Suffering." *Research in Science Education* 32 (2002): 215–40. https://doi.org/10.1023/A:1016030212572.

Roth, Wolff-Michael. "Editorial: On Editing and Being an Editor." *Cultural Studies of Science Education* 1 (2006): 209–17. https://doi.org/10.1007/s11422-006-9024-y.

Ryan, Ann Marie. "How May I Help You? Editing as Service." In *Opening the Black Box of Editorship*, edited by Yehuda Baruch, Alison M. Konrad, Herman Aguinis, and William H. Starbuck, 27–38. New York: Palgrave Macmillan, 2008.

Rynes, Sara L. "Communicating with Authors." In *Opening the Black Box of Editorship*, edited by Yehuda Baruch, Alison M. Konrad, Herman Aguinis, and William H. Starbuck, 56–67. New York: Palgrave Macmillan, 2008.

Sage Publishing. "Increasing Citations and Improving Your Impact Factor." Accessed June 23, 2022. https://us.sagepub.com/en-us/nam/increasing-citations-and-improving-your-impact-factor.

SCImago Research Group. "Description of SCImago Journal Rank Indicator." Accessed June 24, 2022. https://www.scimagojr.com/SCImagoJournalRank.pdf.

Seixas, Peter, and Tom Morton. *The Big Six: Historical Thinking Concepts.* Toronto: Nelson, 2013.

Shear, Sarah B., and Daniel G. Krutka. "Confronting Settler Colonialism: Theoretical and Methodological Questions about Social Studies Research." *Theory & Research in Social Education* 47, no. 1 (2019): 29–51. https://doi.org/10.1080/00933104.2018.1541428.

Smyers, Paul, and Nicholas C. Burbules. "How to Improve Your Impact Factor: Questioning the Quantification of Academic Quality." *Journal of Philosophy of Education* 45, no. 1 (2011): 1–17. https://doi.org/10.1111/j.1467-9752.2011.00787.x.

Suciu, Peter. "Americans Spent on Average More Than 1,300 Hours on Social Media Last Year." Forbes. Last modified June 24, 2021. https://www.forbes.com/sites/petersuciu/2021/06/24/americans-spent-more-than-1300-hours-on-social-media/?sh=7a5371c52547.

Thacker, Emma S., and Aaron T. Bodle. "Seizing the Moment: A Critical Place-Based Partnership for Antiracist Elementary Social Studies Teacher Education." *Theory & Research in Social* Education 50, no. 3 (2022): 402–30.

The Critical Social Educator Editorial Collective. "Welcome to *The Critical Social Educator.*" *The Critical Social Educator* 1, no. 1 (2021): 1–5.

Tsoukas, Haridimos. "Developing a Global Journal: Embracing Otherness." In *Opening the Black Box of Editorship,* edited by Yehuda Baruch, Alison M. Konrad, Herman Aguinis, and William H. Starbuck, 167–75. New York: Palgrave Macmillan, 2008.

Turner, Leigh. "Doffing the Mask: Why Manuscript Reviewers Ought to be Identifiable." *Journal of Academic Ethics* 1, no. 1 (2003): 41–48. https://doi.org/10.1023/A:1025454331738.

Turner, Leigh. "Promoting F.A.I.T.H. in Peer Rreview: Five Core Attributes of Effective Peer Review." *Journal of Academic Ethics* 1, no. no. 2 (2003): 181–88. https://doi.org/10.1023/B:JAET.0000006844.09724.98.

Ward, Amber, Rebecca C. Christ, Candace R. Kuby, and Sarah B. Shear. "Thinking With Klosterman's Razor: Diffracting 'Reviewer 2' and Research Wrongness." *Knowledge Cultures* 6, no. 2 (2018): 28–50. https://doi.org/10.22381/KC6220183.

Wargo, Jon M. "'Sound' Civics, Heard Histories: A Critical Case of Young Children Mobilizing Digital Media to Write (Right) Injustice." *Theory & Research in Social Education* 49, no. 3 (2021): 360–89. https://doi.org/10.1080/00933104.2021.1874582.

Warren, Chezare A. (@chezareaugustus). "Just because the editor(s) don't get it, doesn't mean the work is not good or that it lacks value. #Selah" Twitter, January 5, 2022. https://twitter.com/chezareaugustus/status/1478888976224178177.

Warren, Chezare A., Dorinda J. Carter Andrews, and Terry K. Flennaugh. "Connection, Antiblackness, and Positive Relationships That (Re)humanize Black Boys' Experience of School." *Teachers College Record* 124, no. 1 (2022): 111–42. https://doi.org/10.1177%2F01614681221086115.

Washburn-Moses, Leah. "We Make Tenure Decisions Unfairly. Here's a Better Way." The Chronicle of Higher Education. Last modified March 27, 2018. https://www.chronicle.com/article/we-make-tenure-decisions-unfairly-heres-a-better-way/.

Welbourne, Theresa M. "Editing a Bridge Journal." In *Opening the Black Box of Editorship*, edited by Yehuda Baruch, Alison M. Konrad, Herman Aguinis, and William H. Starbuck, 167–75. New York: Palgrave Macmillan, 2008.

Westheimer, Joel. "The Power of Education." Last modified February 9, 2009. https://www.youtube.com/watch?v=DX1YC5BwGSI.

Williams, Larry J. "Reflections on Creating a New Scholarly Journal: Perspectives from a Founding Editor." In *Opening the Black Box of Editorship*, edited by Yehuda Baruch, Alison M. Konrad, Herman Aguinis, and William H. Starbuck, 188–96. New York: Palgrave Macmillan, 2008.

Zedeck, Sheldon. "Editing a Top Academic Journal." *Opening the Black Box of Editorship*, edited by Yehuda Baruch, Alison M. Konrad, Herman Aguinis, and William H. Starbuck, 145–56. New York: Palgrave Macmillan, 2008.

About the Author

Wayne Journell is professor of social studies education and associate chair of the Department of Teacher Education and Higher Education at the University of North Carolina at Greensboro. His research focuses primarily on the teaching of politics and controversial issues in secondary education, and he is the author of over 100 scholarly articles and book chapters. He is also a two-time recipient of the Exemplary Research in Social Studies Award from the National Council for the Social Studies. In addition, he has published seven books, and since 2016, he has served as editor of *Theory & Research in Social Education*, the premier empirical journal in the field of social studies education.